Before I Could Walk

By

Abigail Collins

ISBN: 0-7596-6642-3

This book is printed on acid free paper.

Scripture taken from THE HOLY BIBLE, NEW
INTERNATIONAL VERSION. ® COPYRIGHT © 1973,
1978, 1984 International Bible Society. Used by permission
of Zondervan Publishing House."

Scripture taken from the NEW AMERICAN STANDARD
BIBLE ® Copyright © 1960, 1962, 1963, 1968, 1971,
1972, 1973, 1975, 1977, 1995 by the Lockman Foundation.
Used by permission.

1stBooks – rev. 5/03/02

For multiples of Satanic ritual abuse who are braving the rigorous frontiers of healing. May you come to know the glory of your Creator, Jesus Christ, and heal in His tender, loving wings.

Acknowledgements

I am greatly indebted to my children, who nurtured and kept me alive during the hard times. I am indebted to my therapist and all the other professionals who treated me, as well as, my priest, other ministers and intercessors who aided my healing.

Last but not least, I am greatly indebted to my husband who extended endless patience and support through this writing project. I humbly give all credit to my Creator, Jesus Christ, who wrote this book for His people. I was only an honored vessel for His higher purposes.

July, 2001   Abigail Collins

Table of Contents

1. Life Before Therapy 1

2. The Day The Party Ended 6

3. Is Ignorance Bliss? 13

4. In The Beginning There Was Chaos 18

5. When The Dam Broke 22

6. Do I Have To Like This Person? 26

7. Don't Forget To Sightsee Along The Way 32

8. Nothing But Fragments 36

9. You've Got To Be Kidding!!! 40

10. A Matter of Touch 46

11. Valley Of The Deepest Humiliation 51

12. Children Are A Gift 55

13. Where Am I? 58

14. Silence Broken 62

15. And Two Makes One 66

16.   Bridge of Acceptance 72

17.   The Longest Night 74

18.   When The Well Runs Dry 77

19.   Where Are You God? 81

20.   Tie A Knot and Hang Tight 86

21.   When Trust Won't Come 90

22.   Don't Quit 94

23.   Masturbastion 98

24.   When Death Had Her Way 101

25.   Help! There's A Gay in the House! 106

26.   Until The Storm Passes Over 110

27.   When The Music Stopped 114

28.   When The Heart Breaks 118

29.   I Just Want To Blow Up The World 121

30.   A Time To Heal 124

31.   Gratis 126

32.   Halloween and Other Significant Dates............. 129

33. Language Relearned.............................. 134

34. Post Integration 136

35. Graduation... 141

36. Life Beyond Therapy 143

37. Bibliography 147

List of Illustrations

1.   Funnyside of the Multiside - "What makes you think I'm afraid?"

2.   Funnyside of the Multiside - "I'm not Multiple!"

3.   Funnyside of the Multiside - "What Do You Mean I Can't Keep Time?"

4.   Funnyside of the Multiside - "This Is Progress?"

5.   Funnyside of the Multiside - "Do I Have To Like These Others?"

6.   Funnyside of the Multiside- "You said To Cooperate..."

7.   Nothing But Fragments

8.   Funnyside of the Multiside - "What Do You Mean These Things Take Time?"

9.   Funnyside of the Multiside - "I'd Rather Fight Than Switch!"

10.   God Rocks Away Our Pain

11.   Integration

12.   "Ain't It The Truth!" - Mt. Healing

13.   Funnyside of the Multiside - "Let Me Out of Here!"

14.   "Ain't It The Truth!"- Sea of Multiplicity

15.   Funnyside of the Multiside - "I'm Ready To Grieve."

16.   Funnyside of the Multiside - "You Said To Loose Control..."

17.   Funnyside of the Multiside - "What Anger Problem?"

18.   Storms

19.   "Ain't It The Truth!" - On The Shores of Normal

Preface

When I was diagnosed with Multiple Personality Disorder, now known as Identity Disorder, there was very little literature available for survivors. I desperately wanted to know someone else had successfully made the healing journey. My mind was full of so many questions and concerns. I felt so incrediably isolated from the human race, as though no one else had experienced my hardships. My therapist gave me clinical material which I hungrily devoured but it didn't provide a road map. There were testimonals with blow by blow, descriptions of the horrifying abuse but I had to know my experiences were coming from myself and not by any outside suggestions, movies or literature. In the midnight hour, I longed for another survivor's assurance of hope and an exchange of successful recovery experiences but there was only a silent void.

This book is a collection of short articles, illustrations and cartoons addressing the various aspects and stages of the theraputic, process of healing. The pages within share the intimate details of my painful journey through recovery with God and my therapist. In a way, it is a diary of conflict and reconcilliation, in a journey of small steps towards trust. It is designed to be read at various stages of growth or as a whole and meant to be tangible proof of another survivor's assent to healing. Provided at the end of every chapter are the Scriptures that benefited me. It is my hope you, the reader, will also profit.

Over the years some methods of treatment have changed due to different schools of thought. Also, treatment is sometimes distinctive to the personality traits of the therapist, not to mention, the intrusion of the insurance company's mandates that now often alter recovery plans. However, aside from those issues and for the record, I personally never experienced any inappropriate touching from my therapist, nor, did she ever make any suggestions to me about the events or those people involved with the abuse. At my own insistence, I didn't permit any kind of hypnotism or drugs to aid my retrieval of memories. I totally relied on God and His Holy Spirit, to bring those buried events into my present day consciousness.

It is my hope, the reader's recovery will be accelerated through this book, as well as, give relatives, friends and support people an understanding of the issues at hand. In no way is this text meant to be a preaching or judgemental platform but an account of my own personal journey into the Light. Every survivor must find their own path and every journey is unique to the individual, although similarities are common to all. My greatest desire is for every survivor to find their own loving, intimate relationship with the real Jesus, so the lies of the false "Jesus", will be banished forever, and you can live in secure, contented peace.

July 2001   A.C.

Chapter 1

Life Before Therapy

One single word could best summarize my life, twenty plus years ago, and that was chaotic! No matter how hard I tried to make the pieces of my life fit together, they fell apart with disappointing regularity.

Exhaustion plagued me most of the time. I had no idea what day it was, except for the school calendar, much less the year. Headaches, painful bowel problems, allergies and asthma were the norm. Anxiety and tachacardia assailed me which finally lead to the diagnosis of mitral valve prolapse. Excruciating, monthly periods totally incapacit-ated my activities for days, until a hysterectomy and reconstructive surgery ended my agony of twenty two years. Apart from the hormonal imbalances, mood swings kept me swinging like a monkey going from tree to tree, often leaving others at a complete loss. Adding to the confusion, I frequently had no memory of my various displays of emotions. Nightmares often robbed my nocturnal sleep and my screams pierced the night for help. Rarely, did I have any recall concerning my night terrors but only a vague feeling, haunted my dreams, from my long ago childhood. Despite my intense dislike of being touched by strangers, I would seek medical help for vague sicknesses, only to be told there were no evidences for my complaints. This resulted in psychiatric referrals that only dead-ended in chemical addictions of tranquilizing, prescription drugs and a large financial debt. Deep inside, there was an unexplainable, undercurrent but no matter how hard I tried, I couldn't penetrate the thick walls of my memory. Approaching my Mother for answers only brought more defeat, as she accused me of having an overactive imagination. An unsettling foreboding left me with a sense of knowing, she held the keys to my truth and was lying. My sense of isolation and mistrust of others was even more solidified.

In addition to all my complexities, my marriage was full of strife and violence that held frequent beatings and child abuse for my two children. Consequently, my children lacked boundaries and were out of control, acting out their emotions. Depression and hopelessness were my constant companions since we attended an interdenomina-tional church that compounded the abuse with "Shepherding". I was counseled not to rely on any other, outside sources and particularly, psychiatrists and doctors. If I left the marriage, I would certainly go to Hell and take my children with me. Accounts of the life-threatening abuse and beatings were cast off in disbelief and ignored since I was the one who walked in rebellion. I was admonished for not submitting to my husband and told I got what I deserved. I needed to repent of my sins, have more faith and trust God for healing. Feeling betrayed by the Church, I held onto God with all my strength. I was exhausted from all the stress and the endless tightrope I walked. I no longer had to be concerned with keeping my figure, as the pounds were falling off with regularity, regardless of my diet and frequency of excercise.

Frightened and alone I wanted to give my children a better life but I felt trapped and unprepared to financially support us. Returning home to my wealthy, widowed Mother wasn't an option, since she on numerous occasions, expressed her hatred for children. I wanted God to magically work an instant miracle and make it all vanish with a happily ever after, fairy tale ending. After a severe beating, demanding medical treatment to my oldest child, I was forced to get counseling from the local women's shelter where I was urged to leave the marriage. Several sessions later, after taking a test on violence, my husband held the highest score, second to one other woman who was paralyzed from permanent, gunshot wounds.

Again, I was strongly counseled to take my children and leave immediately. The woman's shelter had taught me to recognize the warning signs of escalating abuse and it wasn't long before, the tension was building again. This time, however, seemed different, far more intense and violent. Now, my husband was threatening to kill me with a voiced strategy. Chills of terror raised the hair off my neck and arms, as goose bumps surfaced over my body. Reality had hit for I knew this wasn't a scare tactic, using intimidation but a well calculated plan, waiting for an opportune moment for it's execution! As adrenalin flowed, my heart raced, I knew I had to get out and the sooner the better. A week passed but now I was suffering in great pain from a back injury resulting from more violence. Fear gripped my heart like I never knew because I recognized my vulnerability, in my wounded state. I was even more afraid what would happen to the children, as I heard his angry shouts coming from the downstairs kitchen, over pizza. Unexpectedly, a close friend and neighbor arrived, insisting I get the children out immediately or she would call children services. Never, in our history of friendship, had she spoken so sternly leaving no doubt to her timely warning. My life felt like a run away freight train headed for a major crash. I failed to understand why things had gone from the darkest night to pitch black after I tried so hard.

I cried out to God for deliverance. Overwhelming strength and peace engulfed me while I was impressed to get out of bed and prepare for our exodus. I was filled with confirming conviction, there was no turning back this time and God would provide for us every step of the way. He alone would provide the exact moment to flee. A further eruption of rage ignited when my husband read the school notice stating our oldest child's failure in English. Summer school was manditory and it would interfere with, our scheduled vacation! Venting his full rage on our child, I intervened to stop the escalating abuse. Still angered our family vacation would be cancelled, my spouse relented. In the evening, I retired in my youngest child's room, dressed to leave. After dozing off, I was awakened to see my spouse pacing like a caged animal, in our bedroom. The atmosphere was thick with tension, like a bomb ready to explode any second. You could almost smell the scent of violence and blood-shed. Time was critical and I had to make my move now. In the wee hours of the morning, I stole down the stairs, out the front door and over to a neighbor's house to phone for the police. This time, much to my relief, I was believed and there was a police escort to restrain my enemy while I gathered the children and our immediate belongings. As I exited our drive, I knew our lives would never be the same. I never wanted to put my children through anything like this again, nor, did I want a "rerun", of the past nineteen years of marriage. More than ever, I wanted God to lead me to a therapist who could help me mend the broken pieces of my life, so I could eventually have a free, healthy life. There had to be a reason why I was involved in such a destructive relationship and why my life was always on the loosing side. It was definitely time for some major changes and I was more than ready for God to move.

Isaiah 42:16- "I will lead the blind by ways they have not known, along unfamiliar paths I will guide them; I will turn the darkness into light before them and make the rough places smooth. These are the things I will do; I will not forsake them."

Jeremiah 30:17- "But I will restore you to health and heal your wounds declares the Lord, 'because you are called an outcast, Zion for whom no one cares."

Isaiah 50:2 "Was my arm too short to ransom you? Do I lack the strength to rescue you? By a mere rebuke I dry up the sea, I turn rivers into a desert..."

Chapter 2

The Day The Party Ended

"Who braided your hair when you were little? Were your braids tight or loose?", asked this therapist, over the top of her small, reading glasses.

I sat facing my therapist's questions wondering what significance childhood memories had to do with her urgent phone call. Earlier in the week, she had phoned requesting I come to her office, to discuss an important development regarding my treatment. Due to a severe chest cold and rainy, cooler temperatures I declined. Now, I was more than anxious to know what pressing matter warranted an extra session with a refusal of any further discussion, over the phone.

I had entered therapy six weeks prior, for what I believed to be a one-time, childhood issue of rape which had surfaced during my drug recovery from prescription tranquilizers. She had come highly recommended, specializing in abuse issues. The first time I met her, I felt at home in her small, cozy office with no windows. Pictures illustrated by other clients, garnished the walls, in a language that communicated their stories and love. She herself, was an attractive, petite, middle aged woman who wore unique, black slim-lined glasses infrequently and kept her crocheted shawl over the back of her chair. Sunshine and laughter characterized this eccentric, knowledgeable lady and I was captivated by her zest for life. She modeled everything I longed for and pursued. Even more intriguing, was how in the six weeks I had known her, she had taken aspects from my childhood and fit them together into their own, unique design. Now, I was waiting for an explaination from her and to my dismay, she was wasting precious time with a lot of insignificant questions. Inside, I was impatient and growling wanting her to get to the heart of the matter.

Skillfully, my therapist drove home the point I knew very little about my childhood, as well as, other present day events and it was becoming obvious, that I was losing time. Even more disturbing, if I wasn't accountable for events, who was? More to the point, who was taking over in my absence?

Flashbacks from disconcerting conversations whirled in my mind of which friends had described my behavior as childlike or infantile. There was no mistaking, their descriptions weren't of the thirty eight year old woman they knew! Even more frightening, I had no memory of the behaviors they recounted!

"You are trying to tell me I'm multiple," I stated, as I turned from the wall and faced her, looking her directly into her peaceful eyes.

"Yes," was her unwanted answer. Trembling, I staggered to my chair wanting facts and information about my disorder. Numbly, I listened to my therapist, educate me.

"Multiples are highly intelligent, very gifted and talented with an unusually, high ability to heal. They generally are good people," informed my therapist.

Therapy would be long-term, depending on my system with an average time of five to ten years. As if to shed a ray of hope in a hopeless fog, she pulled out her diagnostic DSM text and explained multiplicity was the only disorder with such severity, that was 100% curable. She went on, to point out my headaches, fatigue, chest pain, tachycardia, muscle spasms and drug intolerances were all physical symptoms of M.P.D. The road of healing would be difficult and full of hard work but I could have the reward, of a normal, healthy life.

Still not convinced, I had to be certain she was on the right track. After all, she wasn't the first professional who had misdiagnosed me and for all I really knew, she could be just one more, who would negatively, complicate my life.

"Are you 100% sure about this?", I challenged.

"I'm pretty sure but not completely certain," my therapist honestly admitted.

"What would make it totally certain?" I demanded.

"For me to hear from one of the others. Someone will make contact and make themselves known," my therapist said, very matter of factly.

Now, I was thoroughly convinced this therapist was nuts, yet a tidal wave of fear gripped me that she was right. This whole situation was absolutely bizarre. I was on the threshold of having my world, as I knew it, completely shattered.

Our session was over. My next appointment was scheduled for the next week with additional hours. Weakened, by the chest cold and shock of the diagnosis, I drove home with nerves too frayed to cry. Like a pendulum swinging from one extreme to another, I debated my counselor's proposals and diagnosis. Part of me was convinced she was crazy, yet there was a strange, unexplainable undercurrent of truth to her words. Drained and determined to discover the truth, I flopped across my bed with blank paper and pen on a clipboard, I requested the other persons make their presence known. A flood of tears broke into sobs, as I clutched my Bible praying for God to help me while I was mercifully over-taken with sleep.

I woke rested and for a few lingering moments there was an absence of pain until the memories of the morning's session reeled in my mind bringing an intense sense of doom, along with a knot in my stomach. A thousand questions penetrated my consciousness bringing a determination to resolve the unanswered issues and inner conflict. Reaching for pen and paper, my eyes caught sight of writing which now filled the empty paper.

Waves of shock crashed over me as the truth screamed within: I DIDN'T WRITE ON THAT PAPER... I WAS ASLEEP AND IF I DIDN'T WRITE ON THE BLANK PAPER, WHO DID? With trembling hands, I brought the paper into focus only to discover a blow by blow description of sexual abuse involving my deceased, beloved father, in a totally foreign handwriting. Even more alarming, the story ended with a tiny signature bearing a different identity other than myself.

Panic seized me and gave way to a roller coaster of emotions. Elated I had gotten my answer so quickly, I also panicked with the realization, the therapist was right! Shaking and crying, I held one hand over the other for stability while I dialed my therapist. Fighting to keep in control of my emotions, I was told she was temporarily out of the office and my message to return my call, would be relayed in a half hour. Alone and terrified, I crouched down on the floor, in a corner, holding my trembling body in an attempt to still the raging fear. In those desperate moments, when minutes seemed like hours and hours seemed like days, I was convinced my therapist would ignore my cry for help, as other professionals had done.

The sound of the ringing phone brought me back to the present, while waves of relief gave the needed stabilization to communicate at the sound, of her voice. Through tears and anxious hyper-venilation, I relayed what had transpired since I had left her office, winding up with the written horror story of the past and the terror I now was experiencing.

"Is this what you were talking about? Is this the "other person?", I asked, needing confirmation.

"Yes, dear," she assured, as my sanity was restored.

She quickly explained her limited time, for another multiple was sacrificing her counseling time, so the call to me could be returned quickly. The other multiple had recalled her own painful crisis in learning her diagnosis and wanted to help.

I was strengthened by this stranger's compassion, for I knew I wasn't alone in my daytime, nightmare. My therapist's comforting assurances brought relief to my frayed nerves, as she told me we would get through the tough times together. I had completed a good piece of work. She then, instructed me to be kind to myself and rest. We would resume our work, in our next session.

The years of hopeless wandering on dark trails of misdiagnosis had come to an end, as well as, a lifetime of blissful unawareness. When the other's arrived on the scene of revelation, I became aware of the other secret life they carefully kept hidden and protected for this appointed time of healing. My life as I believed it to be died with the manifestation of my alters. Life would never, ever be the same, rather, my realizations would bring an unforgettable journey of growth and change. Truly, this was the day the party of oblivion and innocence ended.

I John 4:18- "There is no fear in love. But perfect love drives out all fear, because fear has to do with torment. The one who fears is not made perfect in love."

Mt. 10:26- "So do not be afraid of them. There is nothing concealed that will not be disclosed or hidden that will not be made known."

"What makes you think I'm Afraid?"

Chapter 3

Is Ignorance Bliss?

"You are going to have to decide if ignorance is bliss...", said my therapist.

My therapist's words were quickly drowned out by my negative thoughts and self pity. My whole world had shattered and I didn't care about these other people who had so rudely interrupted my life. I was very unhappy with what was happening in my life and with this confrontative therapist. I was uneasy, churned up and stressed out. I wanted to run as far and as fast as I could, from her, my circumstances and my selves. Very definitely, I wanted to escape the bizarre nightmare of multiplicity. Stuffing my hostility and fear, I tried to hear what my therapist was saying.

"Do you want to continue on in ignorance or are you brave enough to face the unknown events of your past and build a new life for yourself?", she challenged.

Hot tears welled in my eyes, as my hostile anger melted to painful fear. How could I tell her my fears of learning about this other hidden life and even worse, my fear of the others who held the keys to this secret world? I was terrified somehow they would hurt me or someone else.

God only knew what had gone on behind my back or what I could be held accountable for. I felt as though I was a living sci-fi monster, cloaked in human flesh, desperately trying to act sane, in a plot of insanity. Feeling isolated and trapped in a web of mistrust, which created a constant overflow of anxiety, I was unable to trust the foreigners within myself or my therapist. I most certainly wouldn't allow her to see the weakness of my vulnerability, as I wasn't fully convinced it wasn't she who was some kind of nut, under the guise of a therapist! I would not break and cry under the pressure.

"The purpose of the others was to protect you. If it weren't for them, you would either be dead or hopelessly locked away in a mental institution. They have sacrificed a great deal for you. It doesn't seem fair that they carry all the burdens and pain while you get off free…. Is your life really so blissful and wonderful or can you accept the challenges of change? You are going to have to decide if being ignorant, is truly bliss. I would like a commitment from you to do your therapy and heal. Our time is up for today. I will see you next week," said my therapist.

I left therapy preoccupied with the issues at hand and drove to my favorite park for a good hike. While walking along the lake and wooded trails, I wrestled with the age old adage of ignorance being bliss, but was it? As much as I hated to admit it, my life was a mess and anything but happy; however, I couldn't recall a time that I ever was happy. There was always an unexplainable, underlying current pulling me down. I couldn't logically account for my mood swings or the deep foreboding apprehension from time to time. I was far from a state of bliss and in view of the escalating proof of the others, it was I who was living in a state of ignorance. Once again, I wanted to run away from my circumstances. Yet deep down I knew to do so, would fail to create a state of bliss and keep me in the darkness of ignorance. It was time for me to take a new path, in a new direction. Despite my negative feelings, I would take the more difficult road and make the commitment for health, to God, myself and my therapist. I was ready to come out of the closet of ignorance and find out about this hidden life. After all, I reasoned, life was full or risks and regardless of how frightening the present appeared, it couldn't be any worse than living with the unidentified pain of thirty eight years. Who knew, I just might accidently get well and end up with a contented, happy life!

Relieved and relaxed with my decisions, I walked on enjoying the colorful fall leaves, on the wooded trail. Suddenly, I heard a child's voice say, "I like pink." Startled, I whirled around to see who was speaking, only to find myself alone.

"My name is Susie. I love Fall and all the pretty leaves. Want to pick some and make a bouquet?", she asked cheerfully.

Realizing I was now in contact with "the others", I carefully responded, "Yes, we can gather leaves if you, like. How old are you?" I asked.

"Eight," the blonde haired child answered. Ready to resume her chatter, another very small, soft voice interrupted.

"I like to pick leaves too," stated the soft voice, shyly.

Taken back with the presence of another child, I asked, "Who are you?"

"Nobody," replied the small voice.

"Your name is Nobody?", I asked, thinking I had surely misunderstood.

15

"Huh-huh," she affirmed.

Puzzled I asked her age.

"Four," her sweet, soft voice answered.

Now, it was Susie's turn to inform me. "I take care of her."

I listened and then asked, "Why is your name Nobody?"

"Because I don't belong to anybody and I don't have a family," she replied.

Further descriptions of gross neglect were disclosed by her involving the same family members I knew. Through my mind's eye, my heart was taken with this sad, brown haired, brown eyed, dark complected waif whose small hand tightly clasped into Susie's.

Excited I had established communication so quickly, while convinced I really was nuts, I bustled down the remaining trails collecting bright colored leaves with my two new friends who let out squeals of delight. I had just lived through the reality of altered time and experienced my first encounter with the "other kind".

Luke 10:18-19- "He replied, 'I saw Satan fall like lightning from heaven. I have given you authority to trample on snakes and scorpions and to overcome all the power of the enemy, nothing will harm you."

Jer. 33:6- "Nevertheless, I will bring health and healing to it: I will heal my people and will let them enjoy abundant peace and security."

Chapter 4

In The Beginning There Was Chaos

Trying to adjust to my diagnosis was like experiencing an instant crash landing of "yippies", from another planet, inside my head. My world as I knew, shattered with the landing of the troops of the unknown kind. Everybody was making themselves known and vying for my attention at once. Quarreling would break out among them in heated arguments and I felt the turbulence of jagged nerves, as each one would struggle to gain control. The little ones would become frightened, overly tired and cry bringing even more internal tribulation. While the younger ones were doing their therapy, some of the adults were threatened by the exposure of the truth, creating additional anxiety within the system. Day and night I would hear their running commentaries and opinions of the day's issues and events. Worse yet, there was no "off button", to the television screen or volume inside my head, making sleep a rare commodity. I wanted to scream and run as far and as fast as I could but there was no escaping their presence. Needless to say, I was anything but thrilled over their invasion and the new world they created for me.

I no longer had the freedom to choose clothing for the day because somebody else insisted on wearing something different. This would result in several changes of apparel while time evaporated like vapor and often made me short on time or late for therapy. Franically, I rushed to keep my appointment, only to have one of the "aliens" protest and turn the car into a different direction. By the time I reached my therapist, I had lost all sense of time and was in a state of complete disorganization. Friends would relay to me behavior and activities that I knew nothing about while others would accuse me of lying or standing them up on given dates. Desperately, I tried to appear normal and stable making up logical excuses when in reality, I was convinced I was falling apart and on the edge of insanity. I was terrified these "aliens", would do something to either land me in jail or my therapist would have me commited to a mental institution. One minute I would be functioning adequately only to have a rush of their presence with new memories overwhelming my feelings and emotions. I felt like a freak in a sideshow stuck on planet earth living too close with the encounters of the "other kind." I didn't want to know their stories of past revelations, I only wanted my safe world back.

Through walls of denial I would argue that it was all my therapist. The "others" were her imagination and I insisted nothing abnormal happened in my childhood. On more than one occasion, I pointed out to her I had everything a child could ever want and lacked nothing! The harder I tried to get a grip, the worse the struggle grew. I had to learn to let go and relax with the flow of the healing process. Gradually, in time with God and my therapist's help, I was able to accept the fact that my world, as I once knew it, was gone. As an adult it was no longer in my best interest to control or silence my alter's painful revelations. Somehow we would have to find the bridge to connect our separations and build a new life. I reached for the Hand of God, as I knew it would take Someone bigger than all of us.

Isaiah 41:10- "…do not fear, for I am with you; so do not be dismayed, for I am your God. I will strengthen you and help you. I will uphold you with my righteous right hand."

"What do you mean I can't keep time?"

Chapter 5

When The Dam Broke

Every area in my life the pressure was building. I was convinced I had to keep a stiff upper lip and remain tough in the midst of my trials and painful revelations. To cry would be the admittance of weakness and failure. In my eyes, to allow tears was to break and nothing would ever touch or break me. As pressures grew, I desperately clung to my impenetrable stone walls, for security and defense. I dared not lose any sense of self-control. I had to prove I was strong and beyond being defeated. I was capable of managing my own life, and I didn't need any assistance. After all, my past had taught me in order to survive, I had to maintain perfect control. Failure to do so would have brought certain death to someone else or myself.

Behind those walls of protection, I was desperately frightened and alone. The full impact of being an orphan was a painful daily reality. The family I once believed loved me, in truth, was my deadly enemy. I wanted someone to love and care for me but I was too terrified to allow anyone to get close. At night behind the closed doors of my bedroom, I sobbed into my pillow, in panicked solitude. The outside world seemed dark, forbidding and cold. I spent hours trembling in tearful, fear of life.

Even more threatening was this latest therapist. Her consistent, gentle caring was breaking through my barriers. I was fearful of her and even more importantly, I was afraid to trust her or let her see me in a vulnerable position. The more she reached out to me, the more anxious I became. I was afraid if I let my barriers down she would take unfair advantage of my weakness and humiliate or use it against me. I was like a walking time bomb ready to explode, any moment.

Then the day came when the pressure was greater than my walls of defense and the flood waters of grief, loneliness and pain poured over the walls of fearful self protection. I could no longer speak, as words choked in my throat and tears streamed down my cheeks. I went from my chair, to the floor and to my surprise, my therapist was suddenly sitting beside me extending her box of tissues. I no longer knew why I was crying as words gushed out about being a forsaken orphan, along with all my other fears and concerns. Gently, my therapist wrapped her arms around me, as I sobbed my heart out on her shoulder for the duration of the session. This was the first time I had ever allowed another person to enter into my world of heartbroken pain. The loving comfort I had so fearfully resisted, only proved to soothe and strengthen me. My parched body seemed to absorb her loving embraces of safe touch while my heart drank in the rivers of comfort and wisdom. Feeling like a fool, I apologized profusely only to be assured this was part of recovery and she had been anticipating this reaction.

The end of the session brought showers of praises from my therapist. I had completed a piece of "good work". I had just broken through the negative messages of programming that had resisted all trust. When I tore through that destructive shell, I was able to receive human comfort and for the first time, experience safe touching. I had learned to trust on a new level which paved the way for further growth, in my journey ahead. I left my therapist's office holding my head high in strength for I had overcome the lies of weakness and my perpetrators. I learned only the strong have the humility to cry.

Isaiah 66:13- "As a mother comforts her child, so will I comfort you…"

Psalm 27:10- "Though my father and mother have forsaken me, the Lord will receive me."

Psalm 68:5- "A father to the fatherless, a defender of the widows, is God in His holy dwelling."

Funny side of The Murky side

" THIS IS Progress?"

Chapter 6

Do I Have To Like This Person?

It became apparent these internal others were here to stay and despite my hostility towards them, they stuck closer to me than peanut butter sticks to the roof of one's mouth. The little ones quickly trampled over every line of defense I had and captured my heart. I was hooked by three, tattered waifs while distancing my own vulnerability. As the children were surfacing, other adults made themselves known, creating a colorful and relatively peaceful coexistance. However, my tranquility was short lived with the arrival of Prudence, my internal self-helper. The others had spoken of her and it was obvious she held a position of organized leadership giving her great authority and power within the system. My first introduction to her, brought intense dislike, for she was everything I loathed. There she stood tall and erect, solemn faced, dressed in black with every hair in place. Her mannerisms conveyed an aloofness of proper etiquette and social refinement, along with an air of opinionated self-righteousness which one dared not cross. I looked up to the Heavens and cried out to God, "Why me?"

I didn't like Prudence's incessant chatter or her constant criticisms and corrections of my lifestyle. After all, from my point of view, I was functioning perfectly well without her "divine" assistance, so who was she to suddenly infringe herself on me? When I tried to slumber, she was still awake and functioning, creating great disturbances in my sleep. I was more exhausted than before I retired to bed, the following mornings and I resented her dominating power with her disregard for my fitfull sleep. Who could possibly sleep with an internal magpie that was a workaholic day and night? In addition to her other shortcomings, she was a perfectionist, being meticulous over everything. Our biggest battles would ignite at the clothes closet where she insisted on proper attire of either dress slacks or skirts with coordinating combinations for tops. Outraged at her ludicrous suggestions, I insisted on my faithful jeans and comfortable moccasins. Thus, the fight for control ensued of endless switching and changing clothes. Adding insult to injury, Prudence would tell all she knew from the ups and downs of the week, to my oddest idiosyncrasies, to my therapist. She along with my eight year old alter, Susie, would inform and dominate the entire counseling session only to leave me with the last ten minutes and the bill! I felt torn apart by Prudences's demands and even worse, I just hated her.

"You have to learn to cooperate," instructed my therapist.

I stood facing her, as anger welled up inside me, like a volcano ready to errupt. That was fine for her to say, she didn't have to live with this menagerie or play zoo keeper. What did she know anyway? It was obvious to me, it was she who was on the "far side".

"You have to give and take. Help each other, share and divide time so there isn't a continuance of deprivation," she continued.

Well, I didn't want to cooperate. Besides, I was just mad as thunder at being stuck with the whole mess and I just plain didn't like or want Prudence. Responding to my therapist, I snarled, "Do I have to like Prudence?"

"If it weren't for the others, Abby, you wouldn't be here. They have fought a lot of battles for you and suffered a great deal, to preserve your life. Don't you think it's time to share the burden?", asked my therapist.

I could see Prudence had brainwashed the therapist to take her side. So, here was the gulit trip and pity party which only added fuel to fire within myself. Hot tears of anger and frustration threatened to spill over my eyelids, as I desperately fought to control my emotions. I felt betrayed by my therapist and hurt. Walls of defense went up again.

"Learn to get along. If you would get to know the others better, your feelings might change. Personally, I think they are all delightful." My therapist continued as she brought our session to a close.

Although I listened in polite silence, I wasn't convinced this therapist wasn't nuttier than I was or ever could be! What disturbed me more, was her breaking through my walls of defenses.

Our session was over and in the privacy of my car, I broke down sobbing, begging God to just let me die. The truth of the whole matter, I was afraid to live and afraid to die. Once again, I found myself wanting to run away to escape the terrors of trust and health.

That evening in bed, I tightly clutched my Bible with sobs breaking forth again. I desperately needed to hear from someone bigger and wiser than myself. I begged God to speak to me through His Word, to give me something tangible to grasp. I felt confused and so very frightened. Leaning over to reach for tissues, my Bible toppled out of my grasp and fell open to Matthew 12:25, where I read, "Any kingdom divided against itself is laid waste, and any city or house divided against itself shall not stand." Engulfed in the Light, I was flooded with love and peace, as I understood I couldn't continue to be at war with my alters. God had been speaking through my therapist about learning to cooperate. If we continued as we were, we not only would destroy each other but our lives would be wasted in darkness as our perpetrators had intended. After all, their primary goal was to keep me in bondage and above all, keep me from fulfilling God's purposes in my life. I had to defeat the darkness and not let my enemies win. I also, understood that it wasn't any accident that I found this particular therapist, rather she was God's gift to me to bring about healing and wholenesss. This season of healing was a divine appointment with the Light, out of His tender mercy and love. Obviously, I needed a change in attitude. Instead of fighting with my alters and creating further divisions by bucking my therapist, I just needed to let go of all the fear and let God have His way. There was security and peace that it was His purpose I discover my hidden past. I asked God to strengthen me and give me a heart of love towards the others, so we could live in unity. In the corridors of my mind, I heard the others pray the same prayer.

Significant improvement took place within my system after that evening. We learned to cultivate an attitude of give and take. Prudence and I often took turns dressing for the day. When we absolutely couldn't agree, we split the difference - she dressed half the body and I got the other half! I must admit, we did look alittle bit peculiar but we were content. I knew my life as it was in the present, was not a permanent situation and someday, I would be very different as one whole person. Cooperative and positive communication put Prudence's talent of organizing time to use, so everyone benefited. In addition, there was a commitment from all of us to forge ahead in therapy with the goal of wholeness. We would help each other the best we could to attain that goal. I learned to overlook Prudence's chatter and trust she was functioning for the good of the whole. Later, I found Prudence to be the loving, nurturing mother I never had and my heart broke over her sacrifices for me. Thus, cooperation not only brought internal and external stability but became our first steps of mutual respect, understanding and love.

Matthew 12:25- "Any kingdom divided against itself is laid waste: and any house divided against itself shall not stand."

Psalm 133- "How good and pleasant it is when brothers live together in unity! It is like precious oil poured on the head, running down on the beard, running down on Adam's beard, down upon the collar of his robes. It is as if the dew on Hermon were falling on Mount Zion. For there the Lord bestows his blessing, even life forever more.

" Do I have to <u>Like</u> these "others" ? "

Chapter 7

Don't Forget To Sightsee Along The Way

When I first started counseling with my present therapist, she told me I would need certain equiptment to accompany me on my journey of healing. She encouraged me to get a hot water bottle and a blanket to wrap up in, for the turbulent times ahead, when I would need to feel safe. Although at the time, I was convinced it she who was the different one, there was an unexplainable, sobbering reality that she was correct in her wisdom. Thus, I embarked on my search for the necessary tools for our trip. As I sifted through piles of blanket sleeper material looking for what would become my "safe blanket of comfort", I made the decision that since I was going to undertake this adventure, I would be sure to stop and sightsee along the way. I knew it would be important for me to carefully collect mementos to treasure and the purchase of a pink and white, checkered blanket was my starting point.

As I began to learn about my significant others, I embraced many positive experiences with them in the healing process. We collected valuable stones at the park which now hold precious memories of sunny picnics and hikes on unexplored trails. As the seasons changed, my children delighted in the fall leaves and we used our creativity in making leaf arrangements while we preserved our memories by pressing leaves within book pages. One of my alters had a natural gift of sketching and she lovingly provided pictures of our outings for future preservation. While she sketched, I explored the library shelves on art and began taking in exhibits with a new appreciation of the talent within myself and other artists. I began to look forward to the day of integration when I too, would possess the talent I so deeply admired in her.

During the healing process of the child, who held the gift of poetry, we created an anthology of her work and took in the sights of the famous poets, while wrapped in our blanket, on crisp fall nights. I wasn't aware then, that I was laying a valuable foundation for myself when my own work would one day be published. We experienced many adventures on our excursions looking for the right stuffed animal or doll that would become each child's comfort. I now look upon those toys with many wonderful memories and they are valuable treasures from past days of healing.

I started a book of firsts, where I kept a log of how we experienced our first stages of life. I carefully recorded our experiences of kite flying, new tradtions for our holidays, our integrations, our first tastes of dreams come true, along with a host of other new experiences. Little did I know what a positive tool it would become to combat depression and suicidal inclinations and virtually be our book of life through the turbulent storms of therapy.

Currently, I'm in search of a chest, to store all the priceless treasures. I'm enjoying the sights of unexplored antique shops and country stores. As a result, my alters not only bring back new creative ideas but involve me in new learning experiences of their creativity. If we are unable to locate a chest in a store, we may embark on new horizons and make our own treasure chest and who knows what fresh frontiers will break before us in our quest ahead!

Along with high intelligence, multiplicity generates multiple talents in which creativity can be transformed into a positive channel of healing. It is a challenge for each of us to explore the frontiers where our abilities lie and develop them to the fullest potential. Our perpetrators brainwashed us to believe that we are the scum of the world, but in truth, it is us the fragmented, who hold the jewels of great price in our goodness, our intelligence and our talents. Each of us has the capacity to make our sphere a richer, safer place and give invaluable contributions to the world around us. However, as the healing unfolds and the potential is developed, don't forget to sightsee along the way!

Matthew 25:15- "To one he gave five talents of money, to another two talents and to another one talent, each according to his ability."

Psalm 103:11- "For as high as the heavens are above the earth, so great is his love for those who fear him."

"you said to cooperate..."

Chapter 8

Nothing But Fragments

Life seemed overwhelmingly hopeless. There appeared to be an endless sea of unresolved issues, none of which had any quick fix answers. My life was broken, as I forged ahead through my divorce. Starting a new life as a single parent and assuming all the financial responsibilities was difficult at best. I was stressed to the limit, more often than not. The crowning blow was the recent revelation of my multiplicity. It was as though my world had been blown to bits by an A-bomb. Feeling extremely fragmented and disconnected, I was convinced there would never be any happiness in my life again. More and more alters were surfacing making the mountains of recovery appear unconquerable. I not only felt broken from life's unjust blows but defeated despite the optimistic attitude of my therapist.

The Christmas season only accentuated my feelings, for I could only identify with the shattered Christmas tree bulbs of the world. There was nothing but pieces and fragments. I grieved for those lost, separated parts of myself, often throbbing in agonizing pain. I grieved for those alters I knew and their pain, as well as, for being separated from them. I grieved for what could have been and what should have been. In addition, grief would overtake me as the illusions of my life continued to shatter and the revelation of further truths surfaced. The realizations of my broken, deprived and fragmented childhood brought devastating trauma as I understood the person I once believed I was, never really existed. My self concept and past history had only been a lie of protection, for I was nothing more than a broken puppet on a string, tossed away to the winds of fate by my family. I was broken hearted at the betrayal of so-called "parents", and grieved the losses of the illusions of "family". Every ounce of energy was drained from me, making my feet feel like cement blocks. I not only was drowning in my pain but I no longer cared. I only wanted to die, as death appeared to hold the merciful end I longed for.

Writhing in emotional pain, I went to church looking for a greater strength for hope. To my surprise, there was a visiting ministry that would have the service and it was geared for children with a puppet show. I was definitely in the right place with my two "outside children", and all my internal flock. The service began and the puppeteer started talking about broken lives and broken hearts. He then took out a puppet who had lost everything he had and explained that God would heal his broken heart and put his pieces back together. Piece by piece, the puppeteer added the head to the trunk of the body and limbs. The puppet would be stronger than ever before because God mends all things perfectly. Little by little, as each part was connected making the puppet whole, his broken heart was restored. Finally, the puppet was put back together and he was a whole new creation.

Just as the puppeteer so carefully mended the fractured puppet, so too, does God lovingly heal our wounds. The presence of God was very close reaching down inside my broken heart and shattered life to caress and comfort me, as no human being ever could. Tears of pain were replaced with His oil of peace. The puppet went on to function stronger in it's new life, than before the initial shattering.

I left church that evening knowing in my heart, through my therapist, God was putting me back together and my broken heart would someday be totally healed. I was strengthened and found His assurance of hope, I so desperately needed.

Psalm 103:2-5- "Praise the Lord, O my soul, and forget not all his benefits - who forgives all your sins and heals all your diseases, who redeems your life from the pit and crowns you with love and compassion, who satisfies your desires with good things so that your youth is renewed like the eagles."

Chapter 9

You've Got To Be Kidding!!!

The holiday season was upon us and it was my first Christmas knowing I was multiple and being a single parent. I was still in the throws of my divorce from an abusive marriage and engaged in a hot battle over visitation rights for my children. Struggling to hide my diagnosis from my children increased my stress and sense of isolation. I felt lost and hopeless, while drowning in an overwhelming sea of pain. The happy holidays only highlighted a lifetime of orphanhood and deprivation.

By then I knew there were several significant others but their exact number was still unknown to me. Mixed emotions would toss me to and fro, in waves of anxiety, while I tried to pretend I was like the rest of the world— normal! I tried my best to accept the revelation of the others but resisted and resented their presence. Yet, part of me really did want to know the whole truth about their histories and the exact number of the troops. Curiosity, no doubt, would get the best of me, for I was painfully nosy about this new development that had so rudely interrupted my life. Yet, in a split second, fear would override all curiosity and I denied their existence, while convincing myself I needed to run away. Feeling even more threatened and crazy I would regularly accuse my therapist, she was the one who had the problem, while insisting nothing out of the ordinary happened in my childhood. While the safety of my illusions were shattered, the rest of the world was made merriment singing "Fa, la, la". More often than not, I just wanted to bury my head in the sand and die.

Christmas day came with tidal waves of grief and despair. Desperately, I tried to keep a stiff upper lip for the sake of my children throughout the day. It was their first Christmas without their father and they were hurting too, regardless of the abuse they suffered. Exhausted, I returned to my bedroom for a brief rest only to disclose a neatly wrapped package laid on my bed. Puzzled, I unwrapped the parcel to discover a black and white portrait of twenty-one different people, ranging in all ages and sexes from infancy to adulthood. Horrified, I flipped the picture over to the backside only to hear the others read the inscribed words, "Merry Christmas, Abby!" Excitedly, my inside children began to share themselves and educate me about the others who were complete strangers to me. Dazed, I tried to be attentive to their chatter, in spite of my shock. I felt as though I had just been told I was pregnant with quadruplets, but worse yet, I was carrying twenty-one people inside of me and they sure wouldn't vacate the premises in a convenient nine months!

"You've got to be kidding", I yelled, as the full impact hit me. This just had to be some kind of sick holiday joke. To my dismay, my alters quickly assured me their gift wasn't a joke but loving reality. Softly, I thanked them but I was far from thrilled.

Promptly, in my next counseling session, I deposited the alien's portrait in the hands of their accomplice, my therapist! Her joyful enthusiasm only inflamed my anger

41

towards her. I hated her at times for revealing the others and shattering my walls of innocence. My world as I had known it was gone because of her. After all, she didn't have to live with this mess. Multiplicity was a job that she enjoyed and certainly not a lifestyle. I was jealous of her safe, normal, happy life and yet I knew I couldn't make it without her. Once again, hot angry tears with trembling lips, threatened to expose my vulnerability and pain. In self-defense, I announced there was nothing to discuss. She could have them all and leave me alone.

I felt like a freak in a sideshow. I not only wanted to run away but I wanted to destroy the others. I hated them and I wanted to get rid of them and be free of the whole mess. Over-whelmed with a blinding blizzard of work resulting from their presence, I was convinced therapy would take a lifetime. I felt doomed as though I was a weak basket case because of the large number of alters in my system. My perception of myself was distorted as weird and disgusting. Fearfully, I believed these alters were really evil demons inside of me. No doubt, everybody else saw them all through my life. I was convinced I was the laughing stock of society and the last to know why I was a weird, ugly freak of nature.

"There were as many of you, as was necessary to keep you alive," instructed my therapist.

This was one of those sessions that I listened and she talked.

"Every alter is valuable and important to the whole. Each one, is an asset and unique, bringing special giftings and talents. Their presence and number isn't a sign of weakness, rather strength. Remember, without the others, you wouldn't be here today," said my therapist.

"I feel like a freak in a sideshow," I responded.

"You are not a freak. You can be proud of yourself and the others for not giving up. Not all survivors make it out of the abuse. It takes a lot of strength and courage to do the necessary counseling to heal," said my therapist.

"How do you know the others aren't demons?", I challenged.

"Abby, the others aren't demons. They are all parts of you who carefully preserved themselves and their history by separating, so you could live and someday be free. They are a blessing, dear, not a curse. I don't deny the work ahead and it won't be easy but together, we can win. One step at a time and one day you will have a whole new life you never knew existed. I want you to think about some of these things until our next session," she counseled, as our time came to an end.

I left therapy feeling relieved and uplifted. However, I was still haunted by the darkness of multiplicity and I desperately needed to know I wasn't cursed or evil. Fearfully, that evening I cried out to the God for assurance in His Word. At random, I opened up my Bible to Ezekiel 16, where my eyes were drawn to verses six and seven, "When I passed by you and saw you squirming in your blood, I said to you 'Live! I said to you while you were in your blood, 'Live!' I made you numerous like plants of the field..."

God's loving presence engulfed me, as I realized He was there even in the abuse keeping me alive. I didn't survive the torture because of any human caring or strength but by the grace of God. It was God Himself who created me with the ability to dissociate. I wasn't a freak, for this was the Light overcoming the darkness. I wasn't cursed and evil but a blessed child of the Light! What was cursed and evil were the wretched acts committed against me. My heart soared, as I understood multiplicity was God's way of escape for me during my horrific childhood. My alters were all parts of me, frozen in time when the original abuse happened. Their growth, in a sense, was stunted from the trauma. Now, as an adult, His perfect plan was for me to heal to wholeness. Again, I felt this was my appointed time to heal while I learned the truth of my childhood and that truth, would set me free. Peace, flooded my soul, for God had indeed answered my cries with His blessed assurance. I was assured of going down the right path, once again, in this journey to wholeness.

Romans 8:28- "And we know that in all things God works for the good of those who love him, who have been called according to his purpose."

Chapter 10

A Matter of Touch

The topic of touching between client and therapist is a controversial discussion with divisions on both sides. Every situation is different and there is no all correct way to heal, anymore than there is any all wrong way to mend. It is my personal belief that healthy therapists will hold, hug and nurture their clients within applicable circumstances. A sound therapist is very secure in his/her own sexuality and mature in the ability to define and hold appropriate boundaries. My recovery, benefited greatly from a wholesome therapist who believed in the healing power of touch. Thus, this chapter will relate the positive benefits of touching based on my own personal experiences.

In the beginning of therapy, as devastating memories surfaced, I became extremely withdrawn. I not only felt I was going crazy but felt dirty, invaluable and nothing more than a worthless, piece of trash. My self perception was well below the animal level with a slimy worm, my superior. Words from others were only shallow and not to be trusted. In my estimation, the people involved in my life only said nice things because they felt sorry for me. In reality, they really didn't mean what they said. My therapist's hugs broke down the walls of isolation and false negative perceptions of myself, such as being too dirty to be touched and worthless, etc. Her holding me during those agonizing times of pain, grief and horror not only connected me with the reality of the present but gave me the missing tools of how to relate to my other selves, to God and the outside world. As my therapist nurtured and comforted me, healing was brought forth and I gained the capacity to feel again. This in turn, broke down the high barriers to my alters and opened the doors for communication. Where there was already some limited disclosures between self and alters, communication was expanded and enhanced.

Because physical comfort and normal parental nurturing was often deliberately withheld, emotional and spiritual growth was stunted. My family's brainwashing techniques of physical deprivation, solidified the false emotional language of the cult. Thus, intense fear ignited at any type of gesture directed toward physical communication. Normal boundaries were always disregarded during Satanic rituals, as well as, in everyday family life. Defining appropriate boundaries was impossible having been raised in a home where there were no limits. Closed doors and privacy was invaded on a regular basis, particularly while taking a bath or using the toilet. All family members took advantage of my body while raping me. During their torture sessions, my body was only a shattered puppet for their latest evil pleasure. As a result of the violations to my body, I didn't know where my family stopped and where I began. I had to learn appropriate boundaries with my therapist. Through her consistent, applicable touching, I was able to make the distinction between good and bad touch, as well as, redefine boundaries while putting them into practice.

At first, allowing any touching was threatening and foreign. I wanted desperately to embrace it but at the same time, I was terrified to try. Again, it was a matter of trust and belief. Would my therapist keep her word and hold the necessary boundaries as we had so often discussed or was this another set-up job, designed to trample and humiliate me? I was scared, very scared, for the cautious, gentle ways of this therapist was tearing down walls which made me vulnerable. In time, step by step, I began to relax and absorb her handling. When I could stop resisting and let go with the natural flow of things, I was pleasantly surprised with a new inner calm and greater physical strength, never before experienced. During those quiet times, I found many of my alters surfacing also, to receive the gentle affection they so desperately craved.

Physical touch became the vehicle for relearning accurate emotional language. It was only then I could begin to grasp that love was not violent and touching was not torture or rape. Touching became non-threatening, soft and gentle. My therapist's physical nurturing conveyed the loud message that I wasn't dirty or wickedly diseased. Rather, the negative communication of the past was replaced with positive signals that I was a valuable human being, worth being loved.

During integrations, it was a popular choice by all, within my system to wrap in our pink blanket and integrate in our therapist's arms. It had become an established place of refuge where it was safe to tell the secrets of the past and remember. There we would receive the miraculous comfort we lacked when the trauma originated. Quiet holding while working the integration process, solidified and cemented the union between alter and self. In those quiet moments I found strengthening, restorative rest.

In my experience, touching was the non-verbal language that had to be learned for a complete recovery. Receiving my therapist's physical nurturing didn't create dependency; rather it became the foundational development for normal, healthy relationships and prepared me for the man I would someday marry. Touching brought accelerated growth in the development process. Appropriate, physical fostering was vital in my recovery, as it spilled over into health and healing in my wounded mind, body and soul.

Luke 17:15- "People were also bringing babies to Jesus to have him touch them."

Matthew 9:20-22- "Just then a woman who had been subject to bleeding for twelve years came up behind him and touched the edge of his cloak. She said to herself, 'If only I touch his cloak, I will be healed.' Jesus turned and saw her. Take heart, daughter,' he said,'your faith has healed you.' And the woman was healed from that moment."

Matthew 14:36- "People brought all their sick to him and begged him to let the sick touch the edge of his cloak, and all who touched him were healed."

Jesus rocks away our pain
— and heals —
our
broken mind, body & soul

Chapter 11

Valley Of The Deepest Humiliation

First there was the diagnosis, followed by the discovery of unwanted alters and children that brought a rude awakening to my previous life style of bliss. Adding insult to injury, was the revelation of babies along with their demeaning requirements that brought me into the valley of deepest humiliation.

When reality of the babie's existence surfaced, I felt frightened and trapped with no other permanent exit but through the journey of recovery. Desperately, I wanted to run away from my circumstances, my over populated alters and my therapist. My life seemed like a worse nightmare, than my long forgotten past of chaos. The embarrassing situations of involuntary switching at inappropriate times and the humiliating conflicts of regressive behaviors in public were devastating in themselves. Now, the prospect of having to face my therapist and *trust* her, in that vulnerable state of babyhood, brought overwhelming terror with an intense urge to die. It was as though I was deaf to my therapist's urging to concentrate on the infantile area of work and blind to the realization that the process of nurturing and integration wouldn't be complex or lengthy. Thus, in an effort to escape it all, I withdrew into a valley of solitude only to incur the wrath of my alters who insisted I take over the necessary responsibilities for healing. My alters assisted only when necessary, leaving me to the humiliation of facing my therapist. Biting back hot, bitter tears of anger and shame, I forged ahead with my therapist, terrified of the utter helplessness I was experiencing in the present and of my dark, long forgotten past.

My sessions quickly brought a significant release to the inner tension within creating a tranquil, restful peace, enabling me for the first time to experience an undisturbed, sound sleep. Encouraged by the renewed strength, I plunged into nurturing my little ones by providing everything from naps, taped lullabies for sleep, to soft cuddly blankets for rocking sessions. Consequently, their healing accelerated and their time with my therapist was concentrated on those damaged and troubled areas. It was very necessary my infants overcome their terror of being "mothered", by an outsider and experience the proper nurturing with the freedom to cry without abusive beatings to let go of the painful trauma on their primitive level. I told myself each therapy session this was important work for my healing because this was truly the last time I would ever have to walk through this valley of humiliation. Never, ever would I go through these painful moments again. I determined to do my work thoroughly and completely to put a permanent end to the living nightmare of therapy and the pain of my haunting, dark past.

To break the strongholds of the darkness, I had clergy involved in the babie's dedication to the Light with the anointing of oil, for God to mend their fractured bodies, minds and souls.

Processing the babie's integration was a totally unique experience and foreign to all other integrations. At first I tried to intellectualize and analyze while attempting to stuff crazy compulsions which resulted in intense frustrations and high levels of muscle spasms. After an S.O.S. call to my therapist, I understood the only way out as one, would be on a primitive level; thus, I would need to yield to the compulsions. Now, I would experience my babyhood and know the abuse I suffered as a baby while healing in the freedom of letting go of the pain. The connection between bed, dirty and pain were eventually replaced with normal, clean, safe sleep.

As I viewed the true reality of my babyhood, I unraveled the tangled webs of my poisoned associations. The tremendous power of my mother's negative words and degrading actions held me captive to the lies of my wharped sef-perception. Now, I could clearly understand that bed wetting and being wet wasn't dirty. This was normal for babies, toddlers and young children. What made bedtime dirty and unsafe was the sexual abuse and torture. I wasn't dirty and shameful, as I had always believed rather, the heinous acts forced on me along, with my perpetrator's minds were vile and repulsive. Neither was I filthy and evil because I was automatically aroused in bed, for my body had been conditioned to their depraved stimulation. Only with these realizations could I stop beating myself for being sinful when waves of sexual stimulation assailed me at bedtime. What I didn't know then, was the new associations to bed would be the very foundation that I needed for when I became sexually active in another marriage. Since I could visualize bed and wetting as clean, safe, warm and secure I could view and link these positive aspects into a loving, gentle sexual relationship. For the first time in my life, sex was an expression of love, pure and secure without fear. The primitive work of babyhood held the keys, to the cornerstone for all future developmental processes.

I gained indescribable joy to the wonder of babyhood with a sense of awe at the priveledge of experiencing that one time season of age. There was a closeness to the Light with a deep inner conviction of my own goodness. The Light was my creator and I could comprehend internally on the gut level, my innocence while recognizing my parents held the evil, darkness of guilt. Thus, the spiritual healing combined with the theraputic processing brought a new found strength. What I once viewed as a curse and one of the deepest humiliations of my life had transformed into pearls of the greatest price, far more valuable than gold. With grateful tears that I hadn't yielded to the temptation of destroying my precious babies, I knew I had graduated to another level of maturity; for I had journeyed out of the valley of humiliation and stood tall, to walk on in strength, proudly holding my head high.

Psalm 139: 13-14- "For you created my inmost being; you knit me together in my mother's womb, I praise you because I am fearfully and wonderfully made; your works are wonderful, I know that full well."

Chapter 12

Children Are A Gift

Life was tough. I not only had my issues but I had two emotionally, damaged children. I kept my twice a week sessions with my own therapist and went to counseling with my children's therapist. My internal kids needed special attention also. I felt weighted down in a sea of needy youths. Frequent exhaustion brought additional resentment and rejection towards my inside kids. I viewed them as inconveniences and obstacles. I merely tolerated them while definitely preferring to unload them at the first exit ramp I could find. I was fed up with their gruesome stories, their demands on my time and their overwhelming energy drain. More than anything, I despised their inappropriate switching when their company wasn't wanted, resulting in further humiliation and embarrassment. Upon rejecting the others, I would have pangs of guilt only to crucify myself for my cold heart.

Then one day, as I was reading the book of Psalms, I stumbled on Psalm 127 and read, "Behold, children are a gift of the Lord, the fruit of the womb is a reward. Like arrows in the hand of a warrior so are the children of one's youth. How blessed is the man whose quiver is full of them; they shall not be ashamed, when they speak with their enemies in the gate."

My previous beliefs suddenly were turned upside down as I realized, as a child I was never appreciated or valued. I was a doll to be used and tossed aside. In truth, I was a valuable gift from God that my parents chose to abuse and throw away. I wasn't worthless, I was a gift from the hand of God that created me! It wasn't my fault they rejected the Light of love and followed the darkness. I was still loved and a gift in God's eyes, despite my family's choices. I wasn't a worthless little wretch of an inconvenience as they taught me: I WAS A GIFT!!!

Once I could see the big lie of my perpetrator's treatment of me along with their incorrect values towards children, I could understand what I had once believed came from the pit of Hell. My relatives weren't an accurate mirror of how God, my Father, saw me or felt about me. My parents were sold out to Satan and Satan is the father of lies. How could I expect any of them to speak the truth? It wasn't God who threw me away but my parents. Since God valued me enough to call me a gift and save me from becoming like them, I needed to adjust my views towards my external and internal children, as blessings.

The words of my therapist echoed in my mind, "If it weren't for the others you wouldn't be here, They are gifts of strength, energy, talents and valuable functions to the whole. Each one is a unique and special asset to the whole body. You never want to destroy them, for they are a critical and valuable parts of you, necessary for health." It was then, I understood the destructive pattern, I had rejected my alters, in a less blatant fashion. Essentially, I was carrying on the darkness of abuse for my enemies, by neglecting and withholding attention to their needs. I was throwing away God's gifts too. It was clearly time to stop the cycle of neglect and embrace the precious gifts of God. I truly was sorry for my negative attitude and behavior. I really did want to change. I asked God for forgiveness where I received a renewed mind to value myself as an adult child of God, as well as, my internal and external children. It was only then, that I could begin to properly nourish and fulfill my part of the healing process whereby love and acceptance could make us one.

Matthew 19:134-15- "Then little children were brought to Jesus for him to place his hands on them and pray for them. But the disciples rebuked those who brought them.

Jesus said, 'Let the little children come to me, and do not hinder them, for the kingdom of heaven belongs to such as these.' When he had placed his hands on them, he went on from there."

Chapter 13

Where Am I?

Unfortuntely, I wasn't insane. I wished I had been so the current happenings in my life could be dismissed as a figment of my imagination. All too often, I was captured by my alters and held in a state of suspension. Sometimes, I was unconscious of their activities while in a resting state and other times I watched from afar, yet powerless to take control.

The last I remembered, I was talking to my therapist. Now all of a sudden, I found myself at the wheel of my car headed down a four lane highway! Panic gripped me, I had lost track of the day, year, where I had been and presently, where I was going.

My brain signaled lost which automatically translated emotionally to abandonment. Terrified, I looked for familiar signs but found none which only intensified my anxiety and fear. Suddenly my internal self helper came to the rescue, calming me with the morning's events. Gradually, I stabilized as I recognized the familiar route back from therapy.

In other incidents, I found myself wondering around the shopping center, parking lot without a clue which entrance I had entered or parked. I only recalled trying on clothes with two of my alters and purchasing those items. Fear began to well up into tears of frustration, as I wandered up and down rows of cars, searching for my own. The others, had long since vanished, leaving me with the mess.

Different situations where unknown people came to talk with me, never ceased to leave me speechless. It was obvious, they had not spoken with me, as I hadn't the slightest idea what on earth they were referring to. Anxiety would churn, as I heard my guilty alters laugh in the distance, while I struggled to bear the appearance of normal comprehension and familiarity to people who considered me their friend! Coping with these aliens wasn't easy and brought a definite clash of interests.

There needed to be some definite changes. I took my complaints to our mediator- our therapist. She helped us understand we had all suffered. Our system needed to be built on trusting unity rather than cruelty. If there was an emergency or anyone became suicidal, then suspension was approved in order to save the whole. Creating deliberate fear had to cease for it only succeeded in breaking trust with the continuation of the past abuse cycle. We needed to cooperate and unify.

Enroute home from our session, we established new rules. There would be no more dumping. If there had been suspension, then the suspended party would be eased back in the flow with supports. Each one would work hard at creating unbreakable trust within the system so security would never be breached. The outside world may betray and injure us but we as an internal unit, would strive to build a foundation of loving harmony.

Our resolutions brought a significant turning point in upward progress. The system was far less stressed and enabled us to use our energy wisely. No one felt threatened or insecure, making it safe for all to complete their work with a family of supports, consequently, work and progress accelerated. We learned new defenses from each other bringing an even greater security to the whole. More stability flourished preparing us for the challenges of the day. Together as a family we were overcoming the past with God's grace. We were taking new steps in self-respect, love and confidence which was a new language and the foundation for the healthy whole.

Psalm 133:1-3 - "How good and pleasant it is when brothers live together in unity! It is like precious oil poured on the head, running down on Aaron's beard, down upon the collar of his robes. It is as if the dew of Hermon were falling on Mount Zion. For there the Lord bestows his blessing, even life forevermore."

Chapter 14

Silence Broken

More and more cult memories were surfacing. Generic abuse had been one thing, but the crimes of the cult were another. Faces, places, codes and functions of the cult brought frightening information. Even though I was just a very young child when it all happened, I still knew too much and for the first time, I realized my safety was at risk. I was terrified to acknowledge the revelations I knew to anyone while trust became a monumental issue, once again. I was functioning on "silence", and "trust no one", while I felt the pressure building as I walked the tightrope of old secrets.

My therapist was pushing me to talk the abuse. Intellectually, there was a blurring where I perceived her as "one of them", while my gut became like lead and unmovable. Slivers of reason would attempt to reassure myself that my therapist was safe, but emotionally, I was like a snowball gathering speed down an avalanche and I couldn't put on the brakes. My therapist was wearing down under my resistance. I wasn't deliberately trying to be difficult, as I was overwhelmed with the inability to trust or speak along with a strong compulsion to run. This therapist was asking me to do the unthinkable. I had never spoken these things to anyone. Tenderly and gently she assured me safety of the information. My body felt like a freight train ready to crash into a brick wall, while my heart pounded like a race horse. I opened my mouth to speak only to have tears topple over my eyeslids. Silently, I sat pleading into my therapist's eyes for help, as I shook uncontrollably. I would go from dazed numb to stark terror and panic, before crying all over again. My therapist continued to encourage me to try to make the plunge into speech. Paradoxically, I had maintained their secrets to survive and now in order to save my life, I had to break the sacred silence.

Slowly, I stepped out on the waters of trust and began to stutter words as my therapist anchored me with physical contact. Gradually, information flowed from my lips describing names, faces, events, crimes, passwords with information regarding black markets. By telling, I was reliving the trauma, making my childhood past, very present. I experienced a major, emotional release. The pressure in my body deflated and I was exhausted. As the session drew to a close, my therapist hugged me with praises of having done good work. I could be proud of myself. My homework was rest and relaxation.

I was unprepared for the kickback, or onslaught of programming that would attempt to drown me like a tidal wave. More memories poured into my consciousness with high levels of anxiety. Alarming levels of fear that my therapist was a plant, informing my perpetrators of everything I told, threatened to drive me to the brink of insanity. Rushes of adrenlin would overtake all reason, as fire alarms activated the internal signal to run! I was too frightened to sleep and dozed sitting up, fully dressed, with all the lights glowing. Even then, sleep was short lived, as nightmares awakened me to further panic and terror. I was being assaulted and sucked in an undertow of programmed messages, designed for self destruction. After all, no person who told, ever made it out alive!

Frantically, with trembling hands, I reached for my Bible crying out to God for mercy. Thumbing through the pages, I found Isaiah 43:1-5, "... Do not fear, for I have redeemed you; I have called you by name; you are mine! When you pass through the waters, I will be with you; and through the rivers, they will not overflow you. When you walk through the fire, you will not be scorched, nor will the flame burn you. For I am the Lord your God, the Holy One of Israel, your Saviour, I have given Egypt as your ransom, Cush and Seba in your place. Since you are precious in My sight, you are honored and I love you, I will give other people in exchange for your life. Do not fear, for I am with you."

As I read, my frayed nerves were calmed and I realized God was on my side. He was with me during the original trauma and He was with me this present moment. His Word assured me that the flood waters of terror and programmed messages would not overtake me. He promised deliverance from my enemies and He was already fulfilling His promises to me with the recent breakthrough. To follow the compulsions and run away from therapy would only serve the darkness and let my perpetrators win. I made the decision, to not give in to the pull of the darkness. God was with me and I intended to defeat the forces of Hell. I held fast to His Word and let His power bring me through while I called on the name of Jesus for protection and deliverance. After all, He surely didn't bring me this far only to let my enemies have their way in my life.

Proverbs 18:10- "The name of the Lord is a strong tower, the righteous run to it and are safe."

Acts 2:21- "And everyone who calls on the name of the Lord will be saved."

Chapter 15

And Two Makes One

Just as every individual is different, so are integrations unique to every person. What may be a difficult area for one person could be problem free for another while experiences vary from integration to integration. After successfully completing twenty one integrations, I found common threads throughout my experiences. As I approached my first one, I very much wanted to know another survivor's experiences only to find myself alone with clinical material provided by my therapist, along with my worst imaginations and fears. Hopefully, this chapter will help provide some positive, informative aspects.

Integration for me felt like major surgery to my nervous system. Like two "live", wires that were disconnected and finally joined as one, integration was the "juice", of fusion bringing a rush of emotions, body memory and enlightenment. I felt the current of the one I had integrated, which magnified my senses. My therapist's normal soft voice was so amplified that she had to reduce her tone to a whisper so I could hear her in a normal, tolerable tone. Distant outside traffic could easily be heard while my therapist either experienced a delayed reaction or remained deaf and unaware to the same sounds. My eyes were painfully blinded by daylight, necessitating the need for a darkened room and sun glasses while colors appeared brilliantly vivid. My nerves were frayed and brittle, as my body embraced the trauma of the past bringing agonizing pain in some instances. I also experienced accelerated heart rate, weakness and overwhelming fatigue that required rest. In addition, there was a complete inability to cope with life and the outside world while long forgotten experiences became mine to own forever. Oddly enough, it was a time for laughter, a time for tears, a time for loving, a time for hating, a time for living and a time for dying but a much needed time for embracing it all.

I required extra amounts of protected, secluded time including complete bed rest with the first three days critical for my body to adjust to the massive chemical changes. While enduring the body memory, memories flooded my consciousness keeping me on an emotional roller coaster. It was all I could do to write the gruesome truth and draw what I couldn't verabilize, often leaving me too exhausted to sleep. By the fourth day, the storms of fusion began to clear and I began to experience renewed strength in a slow, steady incline of health.

Integration for me held three phases. The first phase was on impact of our joining whereby we were **connected.** I felt as though we were attached by a long cord that enabled my alter and me to continue seeing and talking while feeling and experiencing each other as joined. Yet, we maintained a separate distance that gradually grew less, as we neared the next phase. This first phase was the most critical in retrieving lost memories, learning the history and purpose of that particular alter. Significantly, it was an important period for finding the pathways of communication and biological functioning. The second phase held **absorption** where my connected alter and me opened our hearts and embraced, as we blended together as one. I could no longer experience any type of "separate" relationship, thus I grieved at the loss of my intimate companion. The self I had once been, was gone forever and I would experience a unique blend of new colors within myself, in this rebirth. The final phase was a **cementing** season. Like laying bricks for a new building, the mortar has to set and dry for a secure foundation; so too, I required a period of quiet, restful, non-demanding season to solidify the foundation of integration that had just been laid. This was necessary for replenishment while the mind, body and soul gelled.

Generally, I found integrations with babies and children less traumatic and shorter duration, than adults who were more complex and overlapping on several levels. Having had three babies all under one year, permitted integration of the three all at one time. The processing required me to grasp my past on a primitive, infantile level and presented a unique challenge processing three at one time.

For my integrations I chose to do most of them in my therapist's arms while bundled up in my safe, pink blanket. Her secure loving arms brought the much needed comfort and assurance as I began a new foreign journey into the suffering my alter held. My perpetrators had used frequent hypnotic sets and spontaneous fusions were frequent at the breaking of those cues.

Sometimes, I needed hospitalization for shock, dehydration and high blood pressure. Medication was used to ease the pain and relax constricted muscles from the body memory. Close friends were added supports in taking care of me when my health failed, thus, I quickly learned to prepare for those special seasons.

The closer I progressed to an integration, the more I wanted to run, run, run! I wanted to flee anywhere to escape myself and present circumstances, feeling damn if I ran and damned if I forged ahead. There was a return to the nightmare of trapped emotions and circumstances. I was terrified of not knowing what to expect with fears of the unknown causing high levels of anxiety, as my worst imaginations overwhelmed me. After I had completed several, I always felt cold feet with pre-integration jitters knowing the painful road ahead. My fears accelerated worrying that something worse than what I had already experienced would befall me. Another alarming issue, was the fear I would take on those distasteful characteristics of those offensive alters in fusion. I didn't want to inherit the explosive rage that my one alter carried, nor did I care to leave my quiet mode to become an ever ending "chatty magpie". My anxiety deepened, as I feared I would leave my heterosexual role and adapt the lesbian lifestyle of my one alter. My apprehensions were quieted with the assurance that there would be a blend and balanced stability.

Integrations will be less stressful and easier to manage when there are prior preparations. The following is a list of helpful hints that assisted me:-

1. Prepare to retreat and isolate yourself, as much as possible for the next few days, from normal activities.
2. Stock up on essentials and take care of regular, mandatory tasks ahead of time.
3. Special comforts such as bubble baths, hot water bottles, blankets, soothing music, toys and rocking chairs should be kept handy.

4. Make sure there are plenty of crayons, pencils and paper for writing and drawing. They are vital for processing your memories. The colors red and black wear down quickly, so get refills if necessary.
5. Child care arrangements should be made if the circumstances warrant.
6. If integration takes place in your therapist's office and there is a lengthy drive, ask a friend to drive you. It is difficult to deal with traffic when you are in such a vulnerable state. Be wise and stay safe!
7. Have phone numbers of people you can call, in case you need assistance. Remember, it isn't a sign of weakness to ask for help, rather a sign of strength!

Is it worth it? YES!!! The health and wholeness I enjoy today was worth the sacrifices of therapy and pain. If you feel you are strapped to the seat of a roller coaster, unble to exit the journey of thrills and fright, hang on—no matter how scary the drops or demented the twists and turns, there is an end which will bring the reward of sanity, health and healing. Go for it, with a sense of adventure and know every fusion will be another step towards ending the pain. Every one holds it's own remarkable experience, so embrace the most unforgettable journey, you will ever make!

John 5:6- "Wilt thou be made whole?"

Integration....
a time For
healing
Loving
Sharing

WhoLeness

Chapter 16

Bridge of Acceptance

As I got to know the "others", the fear and intimidation left me. The "others", became more and more familiar and a part of me, even in our separateness. Our efforts in cooperating paid off in high dividends of trust and intimacy which built the bridge to acceptance and healing.

To my own surprise I suddenly realized I had indeed stopped fighting them, and had joined the ranks in the battle for health and restoration. Even though it had been a slow, gradual transition, it wasn't until my nervous system had reached a significant, quiet calming that I realized change had taken place. I no longer was at war against myself or the "others", rather they had transformed into my closest friends. I was sympathic and attentive to their injuries and needs. Their grief and sorrows became mine, as I shared their load. Instead of rejecting them as a lie, I turned my back on my former lifestyle of denial and embraced the reality of my multiplicity, as truth. I relinquished my fantasies and illusions while taking on the crushing, painful realities. Life would never be the same for me. There was no turning back for I had already journeyed past the point of no return.

My affections had been taken by these little, internal waifs, as well as, the adults who so courageously sacrificed for my survival. I could not and would not betray them. They more than deserved to retire their functions and battles to the whole through integration. Each and every precious alter became a valuable jewel beyond any wordly price and I was committed to them to work for full integration, the key to a healthy lifestyle. We were robbed of too many wonderful years in the past and it was heartbreaking but that didn't mean we had to be defeated by it. No, we would continue to press forward and create a better future for ourselves. With the grace of God and supportive friends, the past would be conquered with a fulfilling life ahead in Jesus Christ.

John 15:12-13- "This is my commandment that you love one another, just as I have loved you. Greater love has no one than this, that one lay down his life for his friends."

Chapter 17

The Longest Night

Sleeping became an exhaustible challenge as I tossed and turned in an attempt to rest. When I was fortunate enough to drift off, all too soon, I awakened in terror from the nightmares of the past. Only the ticking of the clock penetrated the deafening silence, as fear ripped through my body, mind and soul. All too often, the lights went on again and I wrapped up in my trusty blanket and cried in fright. I desperately wanted to be held and comforted. My body ached for human arms of love to encompass me. This wasn't just a bad movie or nightmare that would go away but this was part of me and the frightening life I led, as a child. It was all too familiar now, that haunting, dark terror and my heart raced wildly. I was sorely tempted to get in bed with one of my teenage sons, just to take the chill of death off my icy body but I knew it wasn't appropriate behavior. I didn't want to damage my children with any further complications. Instead, I called the TALK line at our local hospital. Talking to the staff helped me get a grip and stabilize. The sound of another human voice helped shore up my deep sense of isolation. Even after a brief conversation, I needed more. I prepared my hot water bottle and reached for the living Word. It was going to take somebody more powerful than a human being, to separate the past from the present, so sleep would come again.

There in the early hours of the morning, I was calmed and quieted by God himself. I found His tender assurances in Proverbs 3:24-26, "When you lie down, you will not be afraid; When you lie down, your sleep will be sweet. Do not be afraid of sudden fear, nor the onslaught of the wicked when it comes; For the Lord will be your confidence, and will keep your foot from being caught", and Isaiah 57:1-2, "For the righteous man is taken away from evil, He enters into peace; they rest in their beds..." I realized then, how faithful God had been in separating me from my evil family. I found comfort in Jeremiah 31:25-26, "For I satisfy the weary ones and refresh everyone who languishes. At this I awoke and looked and my sleep was pleasant to me." When I feared for my own safety, Psalm 4:2 dispelled the darkness—"In peace I will both lie down and sleep, For Thou, O Lord, doest make me dwell in safety." As I thought about the Scriptures, I realized sleep and rest were gifts from God. Contrary to my past beliefs, rest did not mean keeping a vigilane all night lying in bed or sitting up in a chair, nor was it spending hours tossing and turning in anxious fretting. Rather, resting was that quiet, confident state of letting go into the secure arms of God. Psalm 91, told me my God gave His angles charge over me and He would cover me with His pinions, hiding me in His wings. I had a choice to accept and believe those promises as truth and enter into His rest or reject them as lies and stay fearful in the darkness. I chose to believe the Word of Light and entered into His blessings of rest. When I pictured myself nestled under His wings, peace enabled me to relax enough for sleep. While I slept, I received from God even though I had no conscious knowledge of it.

When sleep was interrupted or disturbed, I was extra kind to myself. A hot cup of herbal tea with soft music or thumbing through catalogues helped distract the pain. There was, however, none to compare with the comforts of God, for I soon discovered it was in those difficult hours, He was the closest, drawing me into quiet communion with Him.

Psalm 127:2- "For He gives to His beloved even in His sleep."

Psalm 91:5- "You will not be afraid of the terror by night."

Chapter 18

When The Well Runs Dry

I just wanted the pain to end. Attaining full integration and completing my final year of therapy was an all consuming goal. Long ago, I had decided I wasn't going to be a perpetual client and somehow I would dredge through the dark, murky issues of recovery, as quickly as possible. I had become a workaholic seven days a week, twenty four hours a day on the issues at hand.

"Boundaries, Abby, boundaries!", instructed my therapist. No one can work seven days a week, in this stuff. The slower you go, the faster you get there."

I stared at my therapist as though she was mad. To slow down in my reasoning would only prolong the agony and delay my goal.

"Pacing is the key. I want you to let me pace you. Week-ends are for pleasure, play and rest- no work! During the week I expect you to be here and if you are sick or exhausted you can't do your work. Remember, the slower you go, the faster you get there," she reminded.

I was too tired to argue and even though I never would admit it, I was too exhausted to be there in her office. I nodded in silent agreement. I would try her methods of madness.

Even with proper pacing, low energy levels with a sense of futility and depression plagued me. Most of the time I felt retraumatized, dazed and battered from the memories. My past was very real in my present and all too vivid. Broken hearted over the betrayal, my spirit was crushed. It was God's love pouring out through my therapist and others that kept me advancing towards health. Many times I tried to rest but sleep failed. Chronic flu and colds assailed me, with an additional poor appetite at best, resulting in further weight loss to my thin frame. Most of the time, I felt too tired to live. Prior to therapy, I had enjoyed racquetball, distance swimming and jogging. My social life evaporated in the seasons and winds of counseling. The tasks of recovery reduced my energy level to alarming levels of depletion and my plate was full as a single parent of two teenagers.

A major part of recovery was learning to nurture and care for myself. When I could ignore past, negative messages of unworthiness to receive and view myself as a precious flower, I then began the watering process. The watering began with eating balanced, nutricious meals along with a regular schedule of getting proper rest. Lack of structure and boundaries resulted in havoc for myself, as well as, for our homelife. To allow myself to become sleep deprived and battle the endless wars of two teenagers was pure insanity. Thus, schedules with curfews were created along with rules for our household.

As I fed my spirit reading God's Word, I found the map to restoration. There in the book of Genesis 2:2, I found even God rested on the seventh day. I was persuaded that if God rested, He probably had a very good reason and perhaps, I should too. Thus, I entered that quiet, secure place of replenishment that brought peace to my soul and health to my bones through meditating on Psalm 23:1-3. "The Lord is my shepherd, I shall not want. He makes me lie down in green pastures; He leads me beside quiet waters; He restores my soul..." In the quiet hours, I found the humble Jesus comforting me back to life, as a tender, trusting relationship was established on a new level. These were precious, intimate seasons of growth. In time, my attitude towards rest and nurturing changed. Rest became a time of refueling and a gathering of new strength taking on a different direction in Isaiah 3:15, "For thus Lord God, the Holy One of Israel has said 'In repentance and rest you shall be saved, In quietness and trust is your strength." When I ceased to engage in the whirlwinds of activities, I found the quietness of His Presence to supply all my needs. In the silent, stillness there was a trustful letting go on my part with His still, soft voice wiping away all my fears.

Gradually, I learned to be kind to myself as I believed God to value me. I watered the ground of my mind with humorous and inspirational films, as well as, light up lifting novels, books and magazines with attractive pictures. I pampered myself with bubble baths and candlelight showers accompanied with soft music. I developed new tastes for pleasure and grew to relish those special seasons of rest. I no longer viewed it as a sign of weakness but rather a necessary part of health. By the time I was restored and returned to therapy, my energy was renewed sufficiently to do the work ahead.

Each person must find their own creative way of watering themselves which will build the foundation for healthy wholeness. Opportunity always knocks when the well runs dry, as creative restoration always brings forth new growth and fresh life.

Matthew 11:38-20- "Come to me, all you who are weary and burdened, and I will give you rest. Take my yoke upon you and learn from me, for I am gentle and humble of heart, and you will find rest for your souls. For my yoke is easy and my burden is light."

Chapter 19

Where Are You God?

The intensity of therapy was growing along with the suffering. Where was God in all this jumbled up mess? How could a loving God let these awful atrocities happen to little children? Even more significantly, why was it allowed to happen at all? What good could possibly come from such senseless, horrific torture and agony? I was angry that my perpetrators were still walking the streets in freedom. The more I struggled financially, the more my anger intensified. I was outraged that my enemies basked in financial ease, at my expense. Adding further frustration, God seemed distant and silent in my storms of rage. Through sobs of heartbroken pain, I believed His silence meant betrayal. Perhaps God was just an illusion and a lie, just as the cult taught. After all, it was as though the Lord had passively permitted the abuse. I felt a sense of betrayal by God since He failed to intervene and rescue me from my childhood nightmare. I wanted God to strike down my enemies. I wanted to see them suffer and pay for their hideous crimes. Why didn't God intervene and stop the violence, in a world gone mad?

Recovery was tough, exhausting work and I deeply resented my life held up over the inflicted damages by my family. It wasn't fair that I was left holding the bag still paying the high price for their insanity. Rage towards my violators welled up inside of me, as I saw their lives unblemished by the truth. Again I screamed, "Where are you God? How long will the wicked prosper while the innocent grapple for their next breath?

At times I thought I would die trying to do the the theraputic work. The endless pain day after day with all the numerous inconveniences, the lowered immune system from the stress resulting in chronic physical problems, the isolation, and the financial burdens of counseling, not to mention the endless hours of energy invested into doing the necessary recovery work. My therapist didn't tell me recovery would be like this. I never dreamed there would be such a high price attached to healthy wholeness. Why didn't God just snap His fingers and take it all away? Just one touch and He could heal me. It wasn't fair I had to relive the trauma twice in one lifetime. I cried out to God again, "Where are you?" I desperately wanted an instant pudding fix for all my woes.

Only with time and persistant spiritual work I found the answers to my cries. Gradually, I came to understand that God wasn't a controlling puppeteer or manipulator. Unlike the character of Satan, God gave man a free will, to choose life or death. Because of the overwhelming pain and trauma, I couldn't feel God's presence and when I couldn't feel Him, I believed He abandoned me. I did not understand that God's helping hand wasn't based on my feelings. Rather, when He seemed most distant and silent was the very time He no longer walked by my side but carried me in His loving arms. As I continued to read the truth in my Bible, I soon found the truth exposing the lies of my perpetrators.

In Mark 10:13-16, I read, "People were bringing little children to Jesus to have him touch them, but the disciples rebuked them. When Jesus saw this, he was indignant. He said to them, "Let the little children come to me, and do not hinder them, for the kingdom of God belongs to such as these. I tell you the truth, anyone who will not receive the kingdom of God like a little child will never enter it.' And he took the children in his arms, put his hands to them and blessed them." It was there I discovered Jesus accepted me, loved me and did not condone adults neglecting or abusing children. No doubt, since children were special to the heart of God, my suffering had indeed brought Him pain. Jesus wasn't evil and my enemy, as the cult had indoctrinated; rather, He was a God full of mercy, light and love. God's punishment of child abusers became evident in Luke 17:1-2, "It is inevitable that stumbling blocks should come, but woe to him through whom they come! It would be better for him if a millstone were hung around his neck and he were thrown in the sea, than he should cause one of these little ones to stumble." God was the defender of little children and His face was and still is against child molesters. Isaiah 46: 3-4, would comfort and affirm this truth, as I read, "Listen to me, O house of Jacob, all you who remain of the house of Israel, you whom I have upheld since you were conceived, and have carried since your birth. Even to your old age and gray hairs I am he who will sustain you. I have made you and I will carry you; I will sustain you and I will rescue you." Where was God? He was there all the time, through it all. As I continued to ponder the realities of God, I realized what an incredible way of escape He designed through multiplicity. It was His ingenious plan to protect and preserve my life. Now, when I was mature enough to withstand the truth, He was restoring me. In the end, He had already defeated my enemies.

All through the Bible people endured hardships and suffered unjustly. Even Jesus suffered at the hands of the darkness, was betrayed and tortured to death. He knew first hand my pain. I wasn't alone or unique. If not here on earth there would be a payday someday for my abusers. It wasn't my responsibility to punish those who hurt me but it was my responsibility to let go of the rage and vengeance, so God could even the score. After all, He could punish far better than I ever could.

At an early age my violators taunted and mocked me during their torturous rituals and asked, "If there really is a God why doesn't He save you? See, God *is* dead and even if he wasn't, he doesn't care about you! Since children are vulnerable, a part of me believed I was separated from God. It wasn't until I found Romans 8:35-39, that the lie shattered. It reads as follows, "Who shall separate us from the love of Christ? Shall trouble or hardship or persecution or famine or nakedness or danger or sword? As it is written: For your sake we face death all day long, we are considered as sheep to be slaughtered. No, in all things we are more than conquerors through Him who loved us. For I am convinced that neither death nor life, neither angels nor demons, enlighten the present nor the future, nor any powers, enlighten height nor depth, nor anything else in all creation, will be able to separate us from the love of God that is in Christ Jesus our Lord." Where was God? He was there all the time. His miraculous love kept me alive in my youth, He was with me in my present circumstances and He would gently lead me into the future.

Psalm 138:7- "Though I walk in the midst of trouble, you preserve my life, you stretch out your hand against the anger of my foes, with your right hand you save me.

Chapter 20

Tie A Knot and Hang Tight

Unsteadily my hands grappled for the phone while I dialed my therapist. Hearing her voice, I burst into tears, "I can't go on—it's too hard," I squeaked in a high pitched voice.

"Yes, you can," she responded firmly. "Why all the tears, Abby?" she gently inquired?

"Everything hurts so bad, I just can't take it anymore. It is never going to end. I'm nothing more than a piece of garbage, anyway. I just want to die." I cried bursting into uncontrollable sobs.

The stress of the work had left my nerves so heightened and frayed that my whole body felt like a viberator. Any additional stimulus only compounded and intensified my condition. I no longer knew how to steer my ship or what direction to take, for I was lost at sea, in unknown waters. I was beyond coping and rapidly loosing my grip. As a last resort, I called the captain, my therapist. It was her job to teach me how to navigate through these turbulent waters. I didn't know what I was experiencing was a normal reaction to past trauma and this was a normal phase of recovery that would eventually pass.

"Abby, I want you to rest. NO MORE WORK!!! This is the time you need to be kind to yourself. Play some of your favorite music, cuddle up with your hot water bottle or take a warm bubble bath to relax. A gentle walk might help too. I want you to take your pastels and just blend soft colors on paper with no specific plan—just let it go on paper. It is important to let pain have it's own way. Don't try to fight against it but roll with it. Feel it, embrace it and then let it go. You can make it even if it means taking things minute by minute or hour by hour. This too will pass. Call again if you need to, otherwise, I'll see you at your next session," advised the captain.

Combining the captain's orders with my own creativity I learned new ways to hang on during those tough times. Trying a warm bubble bath, I let the pain out by blowing bubbles in the water. Pulling the plug, I visioned all my pain swirl in the current, down the drain. Gentle music, in candle lighted showers gave a sense of warmth, as soft flames flickered across the room. The warm streams of water washed away the trauma and I emerged refreshed and relaxed. Fresh flowers in my eating area brought life to my paralyzed senses. Somehow their beauty absorbed my all consuming, dark memories. The presence of their fragrance and beauty helped to stimulate my appetite while driving out the negative imprints of food. Wrapped in my blanket I rocked away the hurt while focusing on nature's beauty whether it was autumn leaves or fresh pine cones. Blending soft pastel colors of chalk or paint also brought a stabilizing harmony. However, there were times when these activities failed to yield relief and only a higher power could extinguish Hell's anguish. I sought the Light of Christ and found His Presence in the Eucharist and anointing of oil. His all consuming Light drove out all darkness in Holy Communion while His healing touch was welcomed in the application of oil, on my forehead. I experienced God to be my perfect healer and was strengthened by His oil of gladness.

Now, I am grateful for the knowledge I gained during those desperate seasons. At my therapist's insistance, I learned to comfort and parent myself, which was an added safeguard of becoming overly dependent on her. I learned new coping skills that continued to serve me well, over the years. I also acknowledged the reality, that my childhood wasn't going to be the only cup of sorrow I would experience in my lifetime. There were no guarantees for a life of comfort in this world and it was unrealistic to believe otherwise. Pain is a part of life and a necessary part of the recovery journey. I am thankful I persevered when I believed I couldn't go another step. The storm's paralyzing suffering did pass just as I was promised. Nothing is permanent and all things do change, even if it is only our mental outlook. It wasn't how perfectly I weathered the crashing waves, rather, how I rode out the turbulence until the cycles of the storm was over. This was another important stone in the foundation and I emerged (to my surprise) with a new strength every time I encountered this phase. The rewards were worth hanging on, so whatever you do, tie a knot and don't give up. Hang tight for this too shall pass!

Exodus 12:41- "And it came to pass at the end of the four hundred and thirty years, even the self same day it came to pass, that all the hosts of the Lord went out from the land of Egypt."

Chapter 21

When Trust Won't Come

Frustrated and angry I threw the bag holding my pink blanket in the car and slammed the door shut. Anxiety crashed over my body like tidal waves while my heart raced and hands trembled, trying to grip the steering wheel of my car. I didn't know why I couldn't do the morning's work or what was wrong. I just had an overwhelming feeling of being trapped and afraid. I drove home with my body tied in knots crying, as muscle spasms chocked in my throat. For some unknown reason, I had reached an impasse with my therapist. Her role in my life appeared blurred and confused. Sometimes she seemed to be on my side while other times I perceived her as my enemy and momentarily, she wasn't safe to trust. I needed to talk to another successful survivor who made the journey and not a therapist who never lived the actual nightmare of recovery herself.

Upon reaching home, I dialed my sister survivor, Janet. I met her through a writing project, via long distance. The book project's acceptance of my work developed into an ongoing relationship with her. Our shared commitment to Christ created a special bond of unity which blossomed into a friendship based on mutual trust and admiration. I often looked to her for guidance and hope when I could trust no one else or believe I could attain total healing. Without fail, she would bring the reality of wholeness home in one way or another using a language I could understand. She not only had survived her original trauma but had successfully made it through therapy intact.

"Hi, Abby. I was just thinking about you," came Janet's warm greeting.

The sound of her voice brought an immediate reassurance as I poured out my heart and frustration of the morning's session. Through tearful sniffs I listened carefully to her valuable words.

"When I experienced those difficulties, I found it to be a trust issue. There weren't any humans safe to me. Only God was safe to trust. When I came against those barriers it was because I was striving to hide something from God. I had to allow those events to surface and then talk to the Lord before I could share those memories with my therapist."

Janet's words of wisdom struck a note and made sense. The conversation ended with her advise to keep going since the healing was there for the taking.

I decided to take her advise. Grabbing pen and paper, I asked God to bring the hidden past to the surface of my mind. I didn't have long to wait before the sordid, ugly truth came to my mind's eye while my pen flowed with ease, as I wrote the events. It was no small wonder I had resisted for it was bad enough dealing with it in the privacy of my own home. Sickened and oppressed with guilt, I took the matter to God. Tears of sorrow flooded my soul as I begged God for forgiveness and mercy. The burden of the past lifted and I was engulfed in His love. His calm assurance told me all was forgiven and I was His child forever; not responsible for the evil sins of my parents. I was released and knew everything was alright again. Once I experienced the merciful compassion of Christ, I had the courage to share the truth with my therapist and complete the necessary work of letting go.

God was more than able to deliver me despite my protective walls, using His awesome presence, my sister survivor and my therapist. The keys I searched for came through numerous vessels but I found God was the only way when trust wouldn't come.

Proverbs 3:5- "Trust in the Lord with all thine heart and lean not unto thy own understanding."

"Let me out of here! I told you I was a happy child and NOTHING happened!"

Chapter 22

Don't Quit

When I first entered therapy, I was six months into a major drug recovery from tranquilizers and entangled in a vicious power struggle to maintain custody of my children, as well as, secure their choice on the explosive issue of visitation. Meanwhile, my children were, by court order, enduring forced visitation with their father. My youngest, a just turned thirteen, was suicidally depressed while my oldest, fifteen, was dangerously acting out his rage. I was also involved with my children's counseling sessions and dealing with my own. My plate was full.

My life was an endless sea of demands and crises that generated high levels of despair and hopelessness, to the point of wanting to give up my children. More often than not, I wanted a one-way ticket to Never, Neverland where the responsibilities of parenthood were non-existent. Frequently, I rationalized to my therapist, my children would be better off with a "normal" mother, in a healthy environment. Through hot, bitter tears I expressed my resentment and anger concerning their needy demands. I was not only angry with life's circumstances but full of self-hatred for even considering those ideas, for I knew in forfeiting my children I would be breaking the innocent hearts of the two people I loved the most, thus, perpetuate the abandonment, betrayal, and issues of broken trust. During those stressful times, my therapist reminded me that all parents want out at one time or another and cautioned about making a major decision I would later regret. She always encouraged my parenting skills and gently reminded me that one day this would pass.

In time, my therapist enlisted my children's aid, regarding my diagnosis which resulted in opposite responses. While my youngest child was supportive, creative and eager to learn, my oldest was outraged, repulsed and rejected any form of cooperation. Walls of hatred, rebellion and defiance towards my therapist and myself became the norm in this child's hostile behavior. The support and acceptance of my youngest child, helped me weather the storms of rejection from my oldest youth. Slowly, on rare occasions, my oldest joined his brother to help nurture my inside children. Oddly enough, it was my "outside", kids who accelerated the healing process as they they taught me how to live again through their love, laughter and their exciting capers. What I perceived to be insurmountable obstacles in my life turned out to be one of my richest blessings.

Three years later, my life was free from all tranquilizing and mood altering drugs, the divorce was settled granting me custody and my children had the freedom to choose visitation on their terms and my "inside" children were all safely integrated, reducing my system to four adults. I traded my self-hatred for self-respect and love which spills over into the lives of my children. Even more importantly, I taught my children to be overcomers in life's most difficult circumstances through my daily example of commitment to them. I enjoy my children now more than I dreamed possible and I look forward to the years ahead, as we reward ourselves for those lost years and time spent working through the painful Hell.

Do I still have trying times with my children? Yes, I do, just like every other single parent with teenagers. My oldest continues to be strong willed and difficult and my youngest is generally easier but not without the storms of adolesence. Do I still want to leave them? Only for a rest period, to break the burden of all the responsibilities. The difference now is I believe in myself for nobody else can love and nurture them as I can. I'm determined to give them what I never had—that special bond between parent and child that results from the gift of a loving, responsible, commited parent. I will not be like my perpetrators and follow in their footsteps. I'm glad I didn't give up for I recognize the storms of crises and pain, do pass and rainbows of healing often follow. Don't Quit!

Romans 2:6- "God will give to each person according to what he has done. To those who by persistence in doing good seek glory, honor and immorality, he will give eternal life."

Rev. 3:21- "To him who overcomes I will give the right to sit with me on my throne, just as I overcame and sat down with my Father on his throne. He who has an ear, let him hear what the Spirit says to the churches."

1 John 5:5- "This is the victory that has overcome the world, even our faith. Who is it that overcomes the world? Only he who believes that Jesus is the son of God.

Chapter 23

Masturbastion

One of the most pressing and guilt-ridden issues during my recovery of ritual abuse was masturbation. I was in a constant state of sexual stimulation resulting from the retrieval of memories. The harder my system worked and the more memories I received, the more difficult it became to cope with the building tension and stress within my body. Keeping a stiff upper-lip of silence, I braved the rigors of therapy only to return home in severe mental and physical anguish. My underpants and clothing were soaked with unwanted discharge and I viewed my body as a dirty, stinking piece of garbage which was once again out of control. My body felt like it was a bomb ready to explode, while my religious background crucified me with guilt for even THINKING of touching myself. I didn't want to feel as I did, for I was repulsed by the ugly, sexual acts forced on me. Mentally and spiritually I rejected those acts as sin and I felt as though my body betrayed me with stimulation. The sexual stimulation in my thinking translated into enjoyment and pleasure, condoning and accepting the abuse, rather than resisting it. In a sense, my mind was at war with my body. I felt cheap, sinful, humiliated and too embarrassed to trust my therapist with my misery. Even after my therapist addressed this touchy subject, giving me permission to relieve myself, I still continued to condemn myself to a prison of guilt and damnation. I truly felt damned if I didn't and damned if I did, in more ways than one.

What I failed to understand at that point of my journey, was the unrealistic expectations I placed on myself and my alters. Rather than viewing my body's sexual stimulation as a curse, in reality was a blessing, for it was the blessed confirmation of my memorie's truths. My body wasn't at war against me but fighting for me and it was only a natural response to the outside stimulus I experienced. The term "body memory", means exactly what it says. The body has it's own set of memories and will manifest the same symptoms or reenact the trauma of the abuse. The physical response of remembering carries it's own language, as physical symptoms and/or scars reappear. My sexual stimulation was a normal response to recovery and not dirty or demeaning.

Masterbation within the context of recovery in sexual abuse issues, falls into a gray area. There is no morally right or wrong answer. I believe it is a personal choice and any condemnation would be spiritual abuse. However, once the healing is complete and maturity has blossomed, there comes a time to put away youthful lusts and childish things but this season should be directed by God, for He alone knows how each one of us are intricately made and only He knows the seasons of restoration.

When I recognized, children weren't made for sexual pleasure and my childhood innocence and purity were stolen in babyhood, I could forgive my myself for the sexual arousal. Recovery was a slow, gradual process of learning to be kind and loving towards myself. Critical, self-condemnation only perpetuated the agendas of the darkness. Peace finally came when I stopped judging myself and placed my life into my Creator's, loving arms.

It was there, I heard Him say, "Everything is going to be alright, just trust me!"

Isaiah 64:8- "Yet, O Lord, you are our Father. We are the clay, you are the potter, we are all the work of your hand."

Chapter 24

When Death Had Her Way

There were times throughout my recovery that I wanted my alters gone. I didn't necessarily want them dead, just gone. I wanted a magical formula that would go "poof", so everything would be fixed without the process. Logically, I deceived myself to believe the old saying, "out of sight, out of mind." I was weary and exhausted from all the work of therapy. In my thinking, the less there were, the fewer integrations I would have to complete. Naturally, my therapist discouraged that line of logic while driving home the point, that each personality was an asset and gift to the whole. I didn't actually try to eliminate them; rather, I just looked the other way leaving the work to the others, instead of helping to shoulder the responsibilities of their needs. My attitude, however, quickly changed when three of my alters died in rapid, succession during one stressful summer.

In a period of four months I had successfully completed four integrations. In addition, I experienced some unexpected, spontaneous mergings which added to my work load. Complicating matters, my landlord decided to sell our residence and issued a deadline date to vacate the premises. Not wanting to interrupt my integration processing, I stalled for time which angered my landlord greatly. I had relocated many times as a married woman but never did I have to shoulder the full burden of relocating myself and I was anxious over the endless moving tasks. I was down to the wire with a week to be out of the house, bedridden with flu and bronchitis and no house! Left with four remaining days and partially packed, I miraculously found the house God intended for us. With the help of many friends, we met the deadline, as we all worked day and night. The following day, after vacating the premises I turned over the keys to an angry, ungrateful landlord who vented his hostility to me alone. Exhausted and intimidated by his threats, I left the property shaken but relieved the moving ordeal was finally over.

In the midst of the moving chaos was my youngest teenager's birthday. When I attempted to bake the birthday cake, in our new home, the stove blew up and disintegrated the cake! Not wanting to disappoint my child, I searched for another alternative in the hot, August heat. In that desperate hour I discovered ice-cream cakes which literally saved the day. A week later following the move, I woke with severe chest pains and shortness of breath only to be diagnosed with exhaustion, bronchitis and pleurisy. I was under strick orders for complete bedrest for the next six weeks with no counseling. Too sick to care for myself, I returned to bed at the mercy of friends and my children. In the midst of my illness, my therapist was relocating her practice to another town. Very soon, she would no longer be available locally but fifty minutes away. Adding insult to injury, she was leaving on vacation for two weeks, putting her totally out of reach. The major stresses and changes added to my fears and insecurities. Additional costs of long distance calls and gasoline were greater concerns. I was terrified of getting lost or stranded on the highway and felt abandoned and cut off from my therapist's support, even though I knew I was one of the few clients she took to her new practice. I needed the strength of my alters to overcome the stress, new adjustments, fears and my health. However, it was during that extra stressful season, my alters began to die.

One alter, age three, died of neglect while two other adults died from physical disorders. Common threads were experienced in all three cases. Shortly before the death there was an overwhelming fatigue and an acute awareness of the sick one's weight. I had to carry the weak one for they were no longer able to function. It was as though I was carrying dead weights on all levels. As their deaths grew closer, there was a sense of death within the system. Last requests with exchanges of knowledge were made. Following the good-byes, there was an acceleration of my heartbeats, accompanied with extreme weakness and then a release, within my body, that brought relief to the physical struggle. My body no longer was over taxed or weighted down. The intense fight for survival was gone after every death, resulting in renewed physical strength. The alter death experience held a lot of similarities to integrations, yet it was quite a different encounter.

Emotionally, there was an overwhelming sense of loss, grief and guilt. I felt like there was a big hole within myself, a void never to be redeemed again. I struggled with a sense of failure and defeat. Adding to the turmoil, a new identity was redefined within the system, as a result of the losses. Comfort came in the knowledge that each were now one in Christ, Jesus, free of all pain. The sense of shock on all levels required a time to heal from the wound of death's damages. The deaths had taken it's toll. I felt sucked under against my will and powerless under the weight of every dying alter. However, freedom from the bondage of struggle brought a rapid rebounding to the whole system.

Heartbroken at the losses, I grew to appreciate and value my remaining alter's contribution on a deeper level. Through their deaths I learned to take greater responsibility nurturing the others and myself. With the help of those remaining, I came to grasp the significance of their deaths. Those deceased, were diseased and sick. They were the weak ones with no hope of recovery and their deaths had been merciful, ending their chronic suffering. This knowledge didn't totally wipe out my guilt but it helped ease my losses. I learned to walk on and grow from past mistakes.

Some therapist's say despite alter deaths, they are still absorbed into the whole, as a form of integration. This theory was not my experience, especially since the talents held by the deceased alters were never recovered. I found the two experiences very similar, yet uniquely different.

John 15:1-2- "I am the true vine, and my Father is the gardener. He cuts off every branch in me that bears no fruit, while every branch that does bear fruit he prunes so that it will be even more fruitful."

Funnyside
OF THE
Munliside

THERAPIST

"I'm ready to grieve"

Chapter 25

Help! There's A Gay in the House!

The first realization I harbored a lesbian in my system produced shock and panic. I felt helplessly inadequate and sickened by the revelation. I perceived my alter's sexuality as a setback and stumbling block. After all, it wasn't as if there wasn't enough work to keep us in counseling for a lifetime. The dilemma became even more compounded by my mounting fears and embarrassment of discussing the situation with my therapist. I felt humiliated and isolated with the complex problems of this alter. I just couldn't tell my therapist. I was convinced if she knew, she would terminate me. Furthermore, I was all too aware of the clashing views between my therapist and myself. Her liberal focus strained and separated our relationship on more than one occasion. Stubbornly, I attempted to deal with my alter by ignoring her which intensified my fears of someday becoming a lesbian or worse, my alter raping me, like our Mother did.

My system began to suffer under the strain and finally in desperation, I began to communicate with this person, name Chris. To my surprise, I found her as fearful of me, as I was of her! Thus, we began to establish a mutual bond of trust. I found Chris to possess a lot of qualities that I lacked and very quickly, I grew to genuinely like her. Somehow, by mutual agreement we worked things out in spite of our differences. I supported her as she exhausted herself letting go of the poison of the past. After her last counseling session, I was told Chris was critically ill. Having already experienced three alter deaths, I was determined to save her. The remaining day and a half, Chris poured out her heart. All the events that transpired throughout her life, her pain and her hardness of heart towards God. Very importantly, she shared how her lesbian activites were an attempt to heal from our Mother's trauma. Chris had built many walls of protection around herself acknowledging neither sex to have safety. Now that her theraputic work was done with our therapist, she requested to go to church. The following day, Sunday, Chris received the anointing of oil at the altar. The hardness of her heart broke, as the scales from her eyes dropped. There in the Presence of the Light, she gave her life and sexuality to Jesus. She no longer needed to cling to old familiar patterns and gave God permission to transform her to His glory. Chris acknowledged her lesbian orientation as sinful only to receive the compassionate mercy of Christ's healing love.

The alter who had been at war with God for so many years found the peace she so desperately longed for in His Light where she became a new creation. All the hate, resentment and bitterness were swept away with just one touch from the Master's hand. God had never mocked or left her forsaken throughout her anguish but lovingly kept her alive for this appointed time of healing.

Rejoicing over Chris's miracle the whole system was elated; however, Chris grew weaker by the minute. I didn't want to loose her now, especially after everything we had been through. I begged her to hang on. She had one last request. I agreed to anything. She wanted to talk to our therapist. I stalled not wanting to disturb our therapist on her day off. Her home phone number was entrusted to us for emergency purposes only. As minutes passed, Chris grew steadily weaker. I swallowed my pride and made the call only to discover she was out. She would reciprocate our call when she returned. I continued to hold Chris in my arms as she lost strength, waiting by the phone. Tears of regret and grief overpowered me as Chris conveyed her final message for our therapist. Holding Chris even tighter, I begged her to live only to have her die in my arms.

An hour later, the phone rang. I relayed to my therapist the events of the day including Chris's message.

"I'm so sorry Abby, and even sorrier I didn't get to talk to Chris. Every multiple has an alter carrying a same sex, sexual orientation. Take it easy and I'll see you soon. Call again if you are in need.

It wasn't until after Chris's death I understood her lesbian orientation was nothing more than an "acting out", of childhood events. From my alter's perception, it was all she knew while having a safe way to obtain loving touch in place of the brutality inflicted by our Mother. I deeply regretted losing Chris but took comfort in the healing power of God, believing she was in a better place.

James 5:11- "As you know, we consider blessed those who have persevered. You have heard of Job's perseverance and have seen what the Lord finally brought about. The Lord is full of compassion and mercy."

11 Corinthians 5:17- "Therefore, if anyone is in Christ, he is a new creation; the old has gone, the new has come!"

Psalm 103:11-14- "For as high as the heavens are above the earth, so great is his love for those who fear him; so far has the east is from the west, so far has he removed our transgressions from us. As a father has compassion on his children, so the Lord has compassion on those who fear him; for he knows how we are formed."

Chapter 26

Until The Storm Passes Over

The blast of cold air was a welcome reprieve for my edgy nerves and sweaty body. I had just finished my therapy time and things had not gone well. I was full of frustrated rage and ready to ignite into a massive explosion. Angrily I canceled my work time scheduled for the following morning. I quit! My therapist was good at her job, too good, and she was deliberately pushing me over the edge to lose control. I was not only terrified of being in touch with all that rage, which appeared to hold such vast, endless power but once again, but I found myself confronted with the inability to trust. Just when I thought I had it conquered, this monsterous dragon rose it's ugly head again. Waves of futility crashed over me as I faced the realization I was still unable to trust my therapist and myself. Paradoxically, I saved my life by maintaining a tight grip on all restraints and now in order to save my life, I had to let go of the controls.

My thoughts raced as I drove home. Canceling my therapy time was futile since my therapist always ignored cancellations under these conditions and besides, my alters would abduct me to insure the fulfillment of our scheduled treatment. The problem was the rage. I had never seen anger restrained, much less violent anger and I was terrified I would hurt my therapist in the process of losing control. Waves of relief overtook me once I pinpointed my obstacle and in uncontrollable sobs I cried out to the only One I could trust for assurnace and strength, Jesus Christ.

While enroute to therapy the following morning we hit a blinding snow squall. Once again, I was frozen in terror when visibility was reduced to zero on four lanes of interstate. I was co-conscious with my alter, Michael, who was driving. I begged him to return home but instead he gifted me with his analogy. Rage was like a blinding storm and the only escape was to drive through to the other side. He shared the principle as God holds the ultimate control on the weather, so He would hold the control through our therapist. What appeared to be an out-of control storm in reality was a false illusion. The reality I had to press through was a normal, hysterical, emotional response to brutal and inhumane stimulus which was never released. I had to allow myself to feel and experience the out-of control emotions, while my therapist held the boundaries for me.

Michael's wisdom supplied me with the needed courage to do the most frightening act I have ever done- let go of the restraints. I had a large cushion where my perpetrator's pictures were taped and I began speaking all the things I dared not say in the original abuse. At first, I felt stupid talking to a pictured cushion but I pressed on. Somewhere, I crossed over and not only screamed and cried but I pounded the images uncontrollably with every ounce of energy within me. Tears blinded my vision, as I lost all sense of time and my surroundings. I had given way to the violent storm of anger while my therapist held the boundaries protecting me against all possible harm.

There was such a vast amount of rage that I had to take breaks to catch my breath while I anchored my hand in the stable grasp of my therapist. After forty-five minutes of ventilating, hysterical screaming and pounding I had released the violent storm that poisoned and threatened my life. I was free! No harm came to my therapist, nor me and the rage I feared lost it's power over me. What I once perceived as out-of control, was in reality in-control and I learned to trust on a new level. I absorbed the words of praise from my therapist and left with a deep sense of satisfaction of a job well done. I slayed the dragon and I was on the other side of the storm, for clear skies and sunshine followed us home.

Luke 8:22-25- "One day Jesus said to his disciples, 'Let's go over to the other side of the lake.' So they got into a boat and set out. As they sailed, he fell asleep. A squall came down on the lake, so that the boat was being swamped, and they were in great danger. The disciples went and woke him saying,'Master Master, we're going to drown!" He got up and rebuked the wind and the raging waters; the storm subsided and all was calm. 'Where is your faith?' he asked his disciples..."

Chapter 27

When The Music Stopped

In all my previous memories I held onto the belief the abuse just happened. It was as though it was just one of those things that couldn't be helped and these distortions were accompanied by a blurred rationalization that all the abuse was accidental. That protective deception cushioned the painful truth and enabled me to cope. When the realization came and I understood the abuse was NOT accidental but premeditated and calculated, my protective walls shattered. As layers of denial crumbled in a heap I saw my family's pleasure was in my pain. Yes, even the shedding of my blood brought them sexual and spiritual pleasure. I did not want to believe my torture was planned and executed for their enjoyment because if I admitted that truth, I had to acknowledge the devastating betrayal of all my family members.

As memories focused into clarity I saw my own Mother standing by laughing while others had their way with me. The ultimate betrayal came when she raped and beat me in our bathroom. It was no accident that we were alone in the house during those episodes and certainly no accident the maids never responded to my screams, for they were paid well for their blindness and silence. Not only the image of my Mother died but the childlike illusions of holding her perfect and precious, broke in my heart. The image of "Mother", fell off her godly pedistal and she became the pedaphile of truthful reality. Once again, I faced the cold reality of orphanhood. The music had not only stopped but it would never play again for part of me died forever with the realizations that "mommy dearest", destroyed the most sacred, intimate bond between mother and child. Devasted, I believed neither sex was safe creating an inability for any human bonding. I could no longer relate to anyone and only wanted to die. Numb and dead emotionally, I felt like an alien to the human race. I was convinced life could never be the same again for all sense of trust had been destroyed.

I didn't know how, but I had to find my way back to the land of the living despite the fact, I just wanted to die. My therapist was now the road block that would not allow me to quit. I took a horrendous fall but I had to get back up and ride the issues of therapy. My safe relationship with my therapist became distorted and blurred in the light of my realizations. Everything appeared to be upside down again and I perceived my therapist as no longer safe. As my appointment for counseling approached I attempted to cancel, only to hear my request denied by my therapist. Very firmly she made it clear under no circumstances would a cancellation be acceptable and she would see me in her office in the morning.

The following morning I was physically sick and very shaky. Anxiety surged through my body as I faced the fifty minute drive ahead to counseling. Everything within me screamed to run the other way. I acknowledged I was seriously wounded and fragile but I also knew I was standing at a crossroad. If I quit and ran now, I would remain paralyzed and wounded. Did I really want to forfeit my goals for health and wholeness? The choice was mine.

My therapist couldn't make me go to her office and neither could she make me do the theraputic work. If I failed to try, my perpetrators would win. After carefully weighing the consequences, I decided to take the necessary risks and forge ahead.

Step by step, I worked my way back to healthy touching with my therapist. Fearfully at first, I allowed her to hold me and I received the comfort and restoration I needed. These were my first steps towards trust and healing. I had reached the core of why I loathed to be touched and eradicated the poisonous infection. Now the wound could heal. My anxieties and fears were quieted, as my therapist held the appropriate boundaries. The old pain of betrayal drained out while I learned new emotional language of healthy, nurturing touch. I also acknowledged healing would take time and these were only the beginning steps.

I probably would always be alittle cautious, alittle more distant or different than others who had never experienced this kind of trauma. I gave myself permission to take things slow and not expect a microwave fix.

Part of my recovery had to redefine God. If He truly was all loving and merciful, why would He permit innocent children to suffer as I did? Since He didn't stop the abuse, perhaps He was a hateful liar, full of the torment of Hell, as the cult taught. Once again, I had the choice whether to believe the Word of God or accept the lies from childhood. Struggling against what felt natural, I clung to the comfort and reassurances of my clergy and therapist, as truth. God did not approve of the abuse and He cried too when it all happened, as He sustained me through the batterings.

When I stopped blaming God for my Mother's evil actions, the bond between the Lord and myself was restored and I had peace. The reality of the whole matter was my Mother chose very deliberately and systematically her evil actions and she worshipped Satan, while she took on his ways. I didn't have to follow in her likeness and I was free to follow my choices in the Light, with my loving God. Just because she made wrong choices didn't mean I had to be like her for she held no power over me, as an adult. I was free to become the woman God intended, despite what was meant for my destruction. I found peace in these revelations and was strengthened to finish the journey with a childlike trust and faith in God.

Psalm 68:5-6- "A father to the fatherless a defender to widows, is God in his holy dwelling. God sets the lonely in families, he leads forth the prisoners with singing; but the rebellious live in a sun-scorched land."

Psalm 72:12-14- "For he will deliver the needy who cry out, the afflicted who have no one to help. He will take pity on the weak and the needs and save the needy from death. He will rescue them from oppression and violence, for precious is their blood in his sight."

Psalm 18:16-20- "He reached down from on high and drew me out of deep waters. He rescued me from my powerful enemy, from my foes, who were too strong for me. They confronted me in the day of my diseaster but the Lord was my support. He brought me out into a spacious place; he rescued me because he delighted in me."

Chapter 28

When The Heart Breaks

I always knew there was something hidden within my dark past but it was as though I kept slamming into an impenetrable, stone wall that blocked my memory. Now, the pieces of the dilemma fit partially together, for the counseling unraveled the complex hypnotic sets and the mixed messages of the convincing, outward front of my family. However, there still was an undercurrent of guilt accompanied by an uneasy sense that something devasting had occurred during my childhood. I could never get clean enough and compulsively washed everything within my grasp. As time advanced in therapy, I began to experience an impending sense of doom. There was a feeling I did something seriously wrong. The truth surfaced slowly; I murdered someone I deeply loved. Frantic over the unfolding revelations, I demanded to know who, why and where from my system. Drifting off into a fitful sleep, I woke with the agonizing memory of my twin sister's death which took place on our eight birthday, in our marriage to Satan. Until this moment, I didn't know I had a sister, much less a twin. This knowledge explained why I was always searching for close sisterly relationships. While memories flowed, I reexperienced the lost, tender, loving relationship. My longing for her once again brought pain and grief. I truly wanted to die as the reality of betrayal settled in my consciousness. Even though I had no other choice but to kill her, I died a thousand times over, sickened by the events of her death. My heart shattered into agonizing pieces for she truly was the only one I ever loved. Unfortunately, my perpetrators knew this too and deliberately made sure the sacrifice would embrace the one dearest to my heart. Intellectually, I knew I wasn't guilty but my gut screamed with betrayal and guilt. Crushed beyond repair, I only wanted to die; thus I became very suicidal in those days of recovery. I was not only overwhelmed with survivor guilt but I truly believed I couldn't ever live a happy life.

Finding my way back and mending was a process without a quick fix. Recovery was painful at best, encompassing clergy, as well as, my therapist. In the secure shelter of their love, I began to experience God's tender love and forgiveness. My therapist frequently held and comforted my tattered, mind and soul, bidding me to live.

Since my sister's remains were used in Communion, I needed to heal from the devastating spiritual damages. My priest became part of my therapy sessions, as the three of us celebrated Holy Communion. My intellect told me the elements were bread and wine but my gut screamed otherwise, as spontaneous heaving followed. Temptation to retreat from the battle, only urged me to press through until I was victorious. I held God's Word as truth and believed in faith, Communion would stay the bread and wine without the dark, lingering shadows. Very often, in church, I would return to my seat unsure if I would lose the contents of my stomach. Consequently, I sat in the back close to an available exit. Gradually, in time, my physical reactions subsided, leaving me with victorious freedom.

As my therapy progressed, I understood I was as much a victim of my parent's diabolical schemes, as my sister. There was no escape for either one of us, especially since we grew up in the fifties. Realistically, she was spared and now with the Lord, in Heaven. I wasn't responsible for her death, even though I was used as the vehicle of death. The act of murder was forced on me against my will. Slowly, I began to let go of the self-image of murderer and replaced it with love. I began to be kind to myself rather than inflict self-punishment and replaced guilt with liberty. Yes, I lost my innocence having known the violation of the sanctity of human life, but there was a reason, higher than my comprehension, that I remained. Whatever God's purpose was, I chose to trust Him, believing His words of Romans 8:28, "All things work together for good for those who love and trust the Lord."

Psalm 30:5- "Weeping may remain for a night, but joy comes in the morning."

Chapter 29

I Just Want To Blow Up The World

Everywhere I turned, I was experiencing anger or frustration. Circumstances in my present life along with recovery issues seemed endless. My anger continued to gain intensity as I saw the enormity of the mess. I was enraged that I still was paying the high price and deeply resented my situation. Internally, I was like a volcano ready to errupt. High levels of energy flowed through mega voltage and I became frightened by the current. Even more frightening was the fact the rage seemed so vast having no end. I was terrified I would loose control and "act out", my violent thoughts and feelings. Impatiently, I wanted a quick fix only to find the healing route took me through the storms, rather than around them.

As therapy progressed, I learned to ventilate my anger in safe, non-violent channels. Focusing twenty four hours a day on my unfortunate plight, only added fuel to my internal raging inferno. My therapist helped me understand the necessity of not allowing my emotions to mount, warning they would eventually spill at a time I least expected. I decided to take her advise and experience rather than trust my own inexperienced judgements. I learned to write and draw my rage, as well as, pound it out

121

in Playdoh. I wrote letters to my violators and MAILED THEM TO MY THERAPIST. Shredding paper and burning it in a safe place was also helpful. Finger painting served as another valuable outlet along with movies and excercising. Gradually, I began to experience relief from the poison, as the wounds drained. Determined to not let it consume and embitter me, I made special efforts to focus on good things, so positive feelings could develop and grow. The rage would come and go in cycles rather than in single events. I stayed very close to the sacraments and trusted the power of God to keep me from sin. In time, I worked through the cycles. The venomous rage was replaced with loving peace and serenity, far more precious than gold.

Isaiah 41:11-13- "All who rage against you will surely be ashamed and disgraced; those who oppose you will be as nothing and perish. Though you search for your enemies, you will not find them. Those who wage war against you will be as nothing at all. For I am the Lord, your God, who takes hold of your right hand and says to you, Do not fear, I will help you."

Ephesians 4:26- "In your anger do not sin. Do not let the sun go down while you are angry, and do not give the devil a foothold."

Hebrews 10:30- "For we know him who said, 'It is mine to avenge; I will repay,' and again, 'the Lord will judge his people.' It is a dreadful thing to fall into the hands of the living God."

Chapter 30

A Time To Heal

Gradually, I stopped fighting against my healing. I came to believe I was in an appointed season of healing and it was God's gift to me. To reject His restorative plan would be sin. It was also, God's plan that I walk in health and wholeness. When I reached this awareness, I quit apologizing and making excuses for taking care of myself. No longer did I need to rely on elaborate rationalizations to myself or others about my healing. I began to view critical remarks by outsiders as their ignorance rather than my failure. I grew less concerned over other's opinions and approval and redirected my focus to my Healer. I stopped beating myself up for the long distance calls to my sister survivor and other close, supportive friends. They were God's gift, as part of my healing and a necessary aspect in the process. Exchanging an attitude of complaint for an attitude of gratitude, I became increasingly grateful for my resources, recognizing some survivors didn't have the same advantages.

I took blankets, dolls, pictures etc. to therapy in a, large cloth bag and held my head high. I learned to cultivate positive and supportive relationships while trying to fulfill lost, childhood dreams. I couldn't undo the past or fulfill every desire but I could effect some changes. Now, it was safe to love and be loved, as well as, reach for those impossible dreams. Now, I could replace the Raggedy Ann doll my Mother destroyed so cruelly with a new one. I set a vacation to the ocean, as a graduation gift following my final integration. For the first time in my life, it became safe to have a pet, so I healed past wounds with an English budgie who learned to talk.

Embracing the Sacraments allowed Christ to heal my torn past. I grew to a greater realization of His all consumming love and power. Little by little, I let go of the big lie of survivor's guilt. There was a reason why I lived and others died. I had a right to live, a right to heal and have a contented, good life. I was now free to be joyful and happy. Only a lie from the pit of Hell said I must be punished, fragmented, guilty or carry the pain of the past. My Creator fashioned me for His divine purposes even though they were beyond my comprehension. My finite mind could never understand the sovereign ways of the Lord. Who was I to question His plan? When I could see His power as greater than any scheme of the darkness, I could rest safe and secure in the palm of His hand. Eventually, I was able to relax and roll with the punches and embrace my healing, a blessed season, as I put the darkness of my childhood behind me, to follow the Light.

Ecc. 3:7- "...a time to tear and a time to mend..."
Isaiah 49:16- "See, I have inscribed you on the palms of my hands; your walls are continually before me."

Chapter 31

Gratis

As I left my therapist's office, I flipped the door shut behind me. The scenerio had an all too familiar ring. More angered at myself than her, I found myself once more in the position of having to loose control. I had resisted her pressure which brought down a harsh scolding. Underneath the anger was intense pain at having her disapproval while I was thwarted in a blockade of fear.

Enroute home, my alter Art, asked me why I couldn't go over the edge. Certainly after three years, trust was long since established with our therapist. I was reminded of the benefits of loosing control while the therapist held the boundaries and other pieces of harder work, that were successfully accomplished. So what was different this time? Feebly, I attempted to excuse myself by expressing fears of others in the agency hearing me. I knew Art wasn't going to buy my expliantions, as the total reason. He would speak to the therapist about my concerns and perhaps make some different arrangement. Now, we were down to the nitty, gritty of the real reasons. I pulled away and admitted my bankruptcy of knowledge. I knew I had to go to God for the reason. Surrounded by His protected Presence, the overwhelming fear surfaced in revelation. I was afraid to let go of the pain because I was afraid it would overtake and consume me. Surviving was holding on, not letting go, even though on an intellectual level, I knew the letting go was necessary for healing. It wasn't until I reached an agreement with the Lord, to let go of the pain that I found any peace.

As the days passed between therapy dates, the pain intensified resulting in high levels of body memory and sleepless nights. I couldn't get to counseling fast enough to put an end to my discomfort. Once in therapy, I began to write key trigger words as I talked and quickly found myself going over the edge. My therapist quickly directed my face into a pillow on the sofa to absorb the noise of my hysterical emotions. Like ocean waves crashing over jagged rocks, my sobs, screams and rage poured out. I was not only out of control but once again blinded by the force of pain's own storm. As I relived the past, my therapist never left my side and as the rain of tears followed, I received her comforting embraces. The waves of pain had passed, the events attached to that pain recalled, and the bottled emotions of the trauma were discharged into the sea of forgetfulness. What once controlled me lost all power and I was free.

It wasn't until I had gotten to the otherside of the torment, I understood that holding the pain was equal to holding on to the darkness. By letting it all go, I was letting go of the darkness and plunging into the Light. I had to fill the void with good things. Now, I was free to walk on in peace. I gained new confidence and trust not only in God and myself but graduated into a new level of trusting others with no regrets for exchanging pain for the gift of life!

1John 4:18- "There is no fear in love. But perfect love drives out all fear, because fear has to do with punishment. The one who fears is not made perfect in love."

I John 1:6- "If we claim to have fellowship with him yet walk in the darkness, we lie and do not live by the truth. But if we walk in the Light as he is Light, we have fellowship with one another, and the blood of Jesus, His Son, purified us from all sin."

John 1:5- "The Light shines in the darkness but the darkness has not understood it."

Chapter 32

Halloween and Other Significant Dates

The month of October was a nightmare. My birthday was early in the month, the following week was the high octive of October and the grand finale was Halloween. Needless to say, I was a diseaster case and in a crisis the entire month. Spontaneous programming activated and resulted in a trust breakdown in the theraputic process. I felt like someone suddenly flipped a switch where I compulsively wanted to run from those I trusted the most. Everything seemed upside down and blurred. The good guys appeared to be the enemies while my true enemies became righteous. Unable to distinguish between the two, I wanted to run since nobody seemed safe. Past memories increased and surfaced. I felt like the darkness was sucking me under, in an undertow beyond my control. The past was in my present trying to destroy me. Very often, terror and anxiety would get the upper hand. I was convinced I couldn't live beyond the next minute and die while engulfed by the darkness. There was only one way out and that was to trust my God and those closely involved in my recovery; however, that at times was the most terrifying aspect of all. I definitely needed a renewed mind and a change of perceptions if I was to survive.

It quickly became obvious the darkness would attack at every opportunity to reclaim my life. I had a choice to allow the darkness, with it's negative programming, to consume and destroy me or fight for my life of freedom in the Light. I needed supernatural strength and wisdom to know the stratedgy of my enemy. I recognized this battle was not with humans but a battle involving principalities and powers. I learned spiritual warfare. At all costs, I was determined to win over the darkness in the curses sent. Thus, I ran for shelter and safety in the everlasting arms of Jesus Christ. When the church doors were open, it was a top priority to receive Holy Communion and if I couldn't physically get there, I made arrangements to have my clergy bring the Sacraments to my home. The anointing of oil, carried the tangible energy of God that breaks every yoke, provided additional protection and strength. Praise music was played constantly in my car and in my home since Satan flees at the sounds. Daily prayer, Scripture reading and using Jesus' name evicted and enforced the powers of Hell to flee. All these habits provided a disaplined, spiritual life that served me well. As I implemented these tactics, I saw the darkness defeated while I stood victorious in His Light. It was through this learning process, I came to believe the Light was greater than the darkness and I could let go of the deceptive lies of the past. The lie was exposed as a powerless deception. My healing accelerated in all areas as a direct result of my concentrated devotion to Jesus Christ.

As I grew stronger, I redefined those significant dates and holidays. Now, I knew the true meaning and pain behind the calendar events. Gone were the days of blissful ignorance forever- nothing would ever be the same. As I redefined the past and present it became my task to embrace the truth with all it's realities, let go of all the negative hindrances and engage in comforting activities. It was time to start making a new history on those dates that once held so much significant power. The cycles of defeating pain, guilt and darkness had to be broken. It seemed like a monumental task to push out the gloom and despair with fresh, new traditions and activities.

As those dates approached, I learned to pamper myself and take extra care for safety. I planned ahead and prepared meals in advance so my work load would be lighter with extra playtime. I engaged in healthy activities and special treats with my favorite people. I started to learn a new language with new definitions, called normal. Gradually, I found a more secure place within myself, as I associated fun events with serious past seasons. In time, I climbed to higher ground, as little by little, the recognition of Satanic dates faded.

Understanding that to give attention to holidays and other significant dates, serves the darkness, altered my focus significantly. As a child of God, I was free to enjoy life. Satan, the father of lies, would always go to any length to kill, steal and destroy my life. The more he could keep my attention focused on the pain and past memories, the greater control he had over me. When sadness and depression were present, I couldn't rejoice in the Light or enjoy the extra blessings God planned for me. Only when I could grasp God as my loving Father, who only held good things for me, could I let go and soar to new heights beyond where the darkness could not touch, into His everlasting Love.

Romans 12:2- "...but be transformed by the renewing of your mind."

II Cor. 10:4- "The weapons we fight with are not the weapons of the world. On the contrary, they have divine power to demolish strongholds."

Isaiah 54:17- "...no weapon formed against you will prevail, and you will refute every tongue that accuses."

Proverbs 26:2- "Like a fluttering sparrow or a darting swallow, an undeserved curse does not come to rest."

Chapter 33

Language Relearned

My therapist and I were having trouble communicating, I would leave her office frustrated and upset, even more distressed than before I went. Why couldn't she understand? What was the obstacle blocking our communication? I ruled out a case of stubborness where two hards heads collided. No, this was something very different. We were using the same words and phrases but they held different meanings. Yes, that was it, she held a different interpretation than I did. The light bulb went on and suddenly I realized I had solved the great mystery that baffled me for many months. With great excitement I grabbed pen and paper writing words and definitions according to the language of my youth. The following equations are just some of those definitions: love was always measured by money; money = love, anger = violence, love = violent sex, violence = torture, thin = safety, trust = control and death, pain = pleasure, distrust = life, disapline = abandonment, abandonment = torture, God = Satan, good = evil, home = prison, and good = evil.

Soon, it became evident, I needed to define, redefine and learn new emotional language. Together my therapist and I wrote definitions and discussed their meanings. In our sessions I progressed to phrases, such as "I love you", which was used as a signal to kill. By doing this, I was deactivating the programming. In time, the phrase, "I love you", came to hold good, positive messages. It was important for me to work with vocabulary lists with my therapist to distinguish and separate the truth from the lies. As I forged ahead, I viewed the process of discarding old language, as a way of tearing down destructive walls, so I could relate to others normally.

I believe it is essential for every survivor to unravel their own coded language so they can develop and grow. The language we learned to survive on isn't consistent with the rest of the world and they hold distortions that are blurred with incorrect values. When corrected and redefined boundaries are applied with appropriate and accurate definitions which result in healing, health and freedom. Relearning emotional language will also enable one to embrace the power of Jesus Christ and tear down the strongholds of the Devil's kingdom. God never intended for His children to be unequipped or deceived but for us to know His power in the spoken Word.

Mark 11:23- "I tell you the truth, if anyone says to this mountain, 'Go throw yourself into the sea', and does not doubt in his heart but believes that what he says will happen, it will be done for him. Therefore I tell you, whatever you ask for in prayer, believe that you have received it and it will be yours."

Chapter 34

Post Integration

In the beginning, my fairy tale healing played itself out to finish in a "happily ever after dream", only to be shattered in the reality of numerous losses and overwhelming adjustments. As an encouragement, my therapist frequently offered the hope of a whole new life and that hope kept me moving forward. However, my vision of a whole new life and my therapist's interpretations were quite different. I held the unrealistic expectation that with my "final integration", I would arrive with instant healing, instant health and after a couple of weeks of recovery, and all further emotional work would be "gravy". I would walk into a whole new life where there would be an absence of my painful past with instant knowledge and success at my finger tips.

Post integration brought massive physical and psycho-logical adjustments with severe depression. I graduated from the diverse ages of multiplicity into hot flashes of menopause, resulting in further mood swings, crying spells and extreme nervousness along with coping with the permanent physical damages. Overnight, I had to learn to adapt to normal functions my alters once did. Feeling alone and frightened in the pain of childhood events, with thousands of questions concerning the present, I felt caught between two worlds with no escape; for there wasn't anyone left to take over for me. I didn't know how dependent I was on the others until they were gone. My isolation deepened as I gained increased awareness of the numerous skills I lacked and what appeared as an endless road of relearning. I was shipwrecked on a desert island called, "normal" with foreigners who spoke an all new and different emotional language alien to my previous life of separation. Overwhelmed by the intense stresses, I tried to dissociate, only to discover my ship of "multiplicity", had departed leaving me no other choice but to socialize and adapt to what I perceived, as new customs of the "natives". Alone on the shores of "normal", I bid farewell to my childhood disorder, recalling the words of my therapist. "Multiplicity is a childhood disorder that gets in the way and doesn't work in adulthood. It only happens through systematic, rape and torture and is a defense or coping skill needed to survive. Those who can't dissociate either die or go insane." There was acute sadness, as I bid my disorder farewell. It had served me well and had been a good and faithful friend through the years. There was an acute sense of aloneness even though I knew I didn't actually loose my other selves. They were all safe inside me as a whole, I just couldn't access them as separate anymore. My therapist's three week vacation only compounded my sense of isolation.

My therapist's return brought an unwanted confrontation over anti-depressants. I believed it was a sign of weakness, rather than strength to take them. There were still alot of negative, spiritual overtones about taking those kinds of medications. It was viewed by many churches as needing deliverance and sign of spiritual weakness. I also, didn't want to get dependent on pills again. However, at my therapist's insistence, I was left with no other choice. I didn't need to be reminded I was losing ground on more than one level for my weight was now down to ninety pounds. When my expectations of wholeness failed to play out in my fairy tale dream and in the time sequence I believed it should have been, I believed it all to be a lie. I felt betrayed by my therapist and cheated.

Adapting to the permanent, physical limitations brought new levels of pain and anger. My alters did their jobs well, perhaps too well, and now I was left with the reality of it all. There was no magic to fix it or take it away. My therapist recommended supplemental body movement as a way to release and channel my emotions through acting out and righting wrongs of the past and present. I began to learn how I functioned as a whole person and be in touch with all the parts of myself flowing together, as one core. I learned to make the distinction between separate and whole. New memory was realized and integrated on the gut level where ingrained programming could be broken and overcome. It helped usher in freedom to react with normal healthy responses. I didn't partake of the spiritual aspects of movement since it held overtones of dark gray areas. I feared the mixing of forces and used what I could and left the rest.

Post integration was a period of transition accompanied by new levels of adjustment and fundamental learning. Full integration was not a quick fix rather, it was a gradual process of new steps into health and a letting go of past patterns. The coping skills I learned throughout therapy became a lifeline in a solid foundation for learning new skills. Treatment won't erase past histories or magically make it disappear, nor will physical disabilities mysteriously evaporate into thin air but the empowerment of the past no longer enslaves me, as it once did. I dominate it by embracing it and letting it go. Integration doesn't assure one of a "happily ever after", life but it gives you the advantage to make one. I now enjoy the fruits of my work in therapy and it gives me confidence to meet the daily challenges of a well adjusted life. I am free to be joyful and lighthearted in life's circumstances, no longer shackled by the chains of the past and that alone has made it all worthwhile!

Matthew 17:20-21- "...I tell you the truth, if you have faith as small as a mustard seed you can say to this mountain, 'move from here to there' and it will move. Nothing will be impossible for you."

Mark 10:51-52- "The blind man said, Rabbi, I want to see.' 'Go,' said Jesus, 'your faith has healed you.' Immediately he received his sight and followed Jesus along the road."

Chapter 35

Graduation

As my therapy time began to get cut back and distanced I was forced to develop new interests and new coping skills. No longer was I living under my therapist's protective wing. I was free to soar and begin to put my life together. The sky was the limit.

I enrolled in college with the intension of finishing for my degree since I had a year and half left. My oldest child's high school graduation was quickly approaching with all the numerous festivities. In addition to those areas, I was involved with a man who wanted to marry me. My life was full, no longer empty and isolated with the past haunting me.

My life was so busy that keeping appointments for counseling was a nuisance; however, I faithfully kept those times. As I sat in the waiting room, I no longer felt safe or at home. Other clients appeared sick, depressed and disturbed. My heart was full of compassion for them but I knew I no longer belonged there. When my turn came and I was with my therapist, I no longer had anything to say, for I wasn't living from crisis to crisis anymore.

Finally, the day came when my therapist told me I was too healthy to be there. It was the moment I had worked for all those years. Yet, in the midst of the elation, I was frightened to be booted out of the security of her nest. I walked with this therapist through the infernos of Hell and after four and half years, I had grown to love her.

On our final day, I had a big lump in my stomach for it was the end of an intimate relationship between client and therapist. This is where I fought the most painful battles of my life and learned to trust another human being for the first time. It was with her that I opened up my heart, started to love again and reached for life. How could I ever say good-bye to her? How could I ever thank her for everything she gave to me? Desperately I wanted to take her into my new life but I knew it wasn't possible. The client/ therapist relationship had to die and I had to know I could fly without her. The apron strings definitely had to be severed. I had to go on and build a healthy life independent of her.

Grief overtook me as I fought tears in our final hug. I knew she too was having trouble maintaining control of her emotions.

"Have a good life, my dear." She imparted.

"I will. Thank you for everything." I choked. As I pulled away saying good-bye I walked out the door, never to return again.

Like a bird set free from an imprisoned cage, I soared into my new life with Jesus.

John 8:32- "Then you will know the truth, and the truth will set you free."

John 8:36- "So if the son sets you free, you will be free indeed."

Chapter 36

Life Beyond Therapy

This was a time for celebration and a difficult season of grief. The long, intimate relationship with my therapist was gone. I felt as though I lost my best friend. So many times I wanted to share the day's happenings with her, only to be jolted back to reality that she no longer was in my life. There were times I just wanted the security of hearing her voice and I was tempted to call but my determination to find my way without her ruled. I had to adjust to life without a therapist. It wasn't easy but I knew I could make it. After all, I reasoned, I had been through Hell and back; surely I could hurdle this final adjustment.

I began filling my time with new goals, stimulating challenges and projects. Funds for school were not in the picture, so I started writing again. Now, with counseling completed I had time and energy to develop a social life. I was careful to cultivate good, wholesome friendships.

Eventually, I remarried and my life went on dealing with normal everyday problems. In time, my children were out of the nest and leading their own lives.

Marriage brought sexual issues not addressed in therapy because I was not sexually active during my recovery. My ability to function sexually didn't happen overnight but was

143

a slow process of gradual, gentle, loving touching. My husband was prepared to wait and take things as slowly as needed. He did not have any great expectations for immediate fulfillment and wisely gave me the controls to lead. Essentially, he took all the pressure off, so I could take our lovemaking as I could tolerate. I was the one who initiated our lovemaking and there was no pressure to end it with sexual intercourse. We took it one step at a time. There were many times, I thought I would never get to a point where we would have a fulfilling, sexual relationship but my love for my husband, kept me forging ahead. I also, remembered the wisdom of my therapist who taught me to conquer my fears and insecurities, so I could always choose to do something and if I choose not to, it wouldn't be because it dominated me out of fear or dysfunction. There were times old shadows, resurrected painful memories but gradually with persistence, we reached the other side of the work and found the fulfillment of our heart's desires.

With passing time and distance, I grew away from my therapist and let go of my insecurities. I found my nitch in the world around me and found my identity in Christ, Jesus. My life was His, to use, for His service.

Psalm 32:7-8- "You are my hiding place you will protect me from trouble and surround me with songs of deliverance. I will instruct you and teach you in the way you should go; I will counsel you and watch over you."

Romans 5:3-5- "Not only so, but we also rejoice in our sufferings, because we know that suffering produces perseverance; perseverance, character; and character, hope. And hope does not disappoint us because God poured out his love into our hearts to the Holy Spirit, whom he has given us."

Jeremiah 33:6- "Behold, I will bring it to health and healing. And I will heal them; and I will reveal to them an abundance of peace and truth."

Abigail Collins

Bibliography

All Scriptures taken from The Full Life Study Bible, New International Version, Zondervan Publishing House; 1973, and the New American Standard Bible; Thomas Nelson Publishers, 1985 New American Standard.

About the Author

Diagnosed with Multiple Personality/Identity Disorder, Abigail has helped pioneer the frontiers of Satanic ritual abuse when little data was available for treatment. At the persuasion of her therapist, she began writing and drawing for publications and became involved in numerous projects throughout her recovery years. Her artwork has traveled throughout the United States to various Mental Health and teaching seminars, as well as, published in several issues of Many Voices. Her work also includes Dr. Walter Young, M.D. and Bob Larson's video, In Satan's Name, where the evils and recovery of ritual abuse are graphically exposed. Several articles within this book have appeared in Many Voices, Healing Woman and *MENDING OURSELVES*. With joy and laughter, Abigail impacts her audiences as she shares her testimony, journey and her Christian faith in Mental Health seminars, religious retreats and youth summits.

Today she enjoys a fulfilling life with her husband and her adult children. A variety of interests hold her attention in the sports of hiking and swimming while she enjoys hobbies of gardening, sewing, collecting Ginny Dolls and shelling. Dedicated to seeing the captive set free and the brokenhearted healed she fulfills her destiny by offering hope and deliverance to the suffering.